gradleware

Gradleware, a valued sponsor of this book, is a services provider that offers both training (*http://gradleware.com/training*) and consulting services (*http://gradleware.com/consulting*) around the innovative Gradle build product. Consulting services range from automation audits to full implementations of Gradle across a build and delivery team's stack of artifacts. Gradleware training offerings span one-day open-enrollment online boot camps to comprehensive three-day hands-on workshops.

> *"Since moving Hibernate to Gradle as its build tool, I feel much more in control of the build, as opposed to the build tool being in control and often getting in the way. In my opinion, Gradle has really nailed that sweet spot between build-by- convention and still allowing build writers to script around their unique sets of concerns."*
>
> –Steve Ebersole, JBoss Hibernate Creator

> *"Concise, practical, powerful—just like Gradle itself. Indispensable in its presentation of the basics, as well as critical topics like Ant/Maven integration and multiproject builds. A perfect resource for teams needing to get up to speed quickly."*
>
> —Chris Beams, SpringSource

T0261054

Building and Testing with Gradle

Building and Testing with Gradle

Tim Berglund and Matthew McCullough

foreword by Hans Dockter, Founder of Gradle and CEO of Gradleware

O'REILLY®

Beijing · Cambridge · Farnham · Köln · Sebastopol · Tokyo

Building and Testing with Gradle

by Tim Berglund and Matthew McCullough

Published by O'Reilly Media, Inc., 1005 Gravenstein Highway North, Sebastopol, CA 95472.

O'Reilly books may be purchased for educational, business, or sales promotional use. Online editions are also available for most titles (*http://my.safaribooksonline.com*). For more information, contact our corporate/institutional sales department: (800) 998-9938 or *corporate@oreilly.com*.

Editors: Mike Loukides and Meghan Blanchette	**Cover Designer:** Karen Montgomery
Production Editor: Jasmine Perez	**Interior Designer:** David Futato
Proofreader: Jasmine Perez	**Illustrator:** Robert Romano

Printing History:

July 2011:   First Edition.

ISBN: 978-1-449-30463-8

[LSI]   [2011-07-12]

1310494891

To my son, Zach, who plays the trumpet

Psalm 150:3

—Tim Berglund

This book is dedicated to my entire extended family who, in numerous ways, facilitated the creation of this first of many books. To my beautiful and supportive wife Madelaine for allowing me long nights of typing and days of constant Gradle talk. My daughters Scarlette and Violette for playing rounds of Angry Birds while I made on-the-road commits to the book. My brother Jordan for promoting Gradle in his circle of Denver developers and supporting my photographic imagery needs in Gradle educational materials. And my parents Terry and Marylyn for bearing the laptop coming out even at dinner whenever a few more paragraphs could be composed.

—Matthew McCullough

Table of Contents

Foreword xi

Preface xiii

1. Hello, Gradle! 1
   Build Files in Groovy   2
   Domain-Specific Build Languages   2
   Getting Started   3
      MacOS Installation with Brew   4
      Linux and MacOS Installation   4
      Windows Installation   4
   The Hello World Build File   6
   Building a Java Program   8
   The Gradle Command Line   10

2. Gradle Tasks 13
   Declaring a Task   13
   Task Action   14
   Task Configuration   15
   Tasks Are Objects   16
      Methods of DefaultTask   17
      Properties of DefaultTask   22
      Dynamic Properties   26
   Task Types   27
      Copy   27
      Jar   27
      JavaExec   28
   Custom Task Types   29
      Custom Tasks Types in the Build File   29
      Custom Tasks in the Source Tree   31
   Where Do Tasks Come From?   32

Conclusion   33

3. **Ant and Gradle** **35**
   The Vocabulary   35
   Hello Ant   37
   Importing Custom Ant Tasks   38
   Complex Ant Configuration   40
   Importing an Entire Ant Build File   41
   Ant Target and Gradle Task Codependence   42
   Using AntBuilder   43
   A Harmonic Duo   46

4. **Maven and Gradle** **47**
   Cue Graven?   47
   The Maven POM and Gradle Build   48
   Maven Goals, Gradle Tasks   50
   The Standard Maven Coordinates, Gradle Properties   51
   More Gradle Properties   52
   Dependencies   55
   Repositories   57
   Unit Testing   59
   Multiple Source Directories   61
   Default Tasks   62
   The Maven Plug-in   62
   Installing to the Local Maven Repository (Cache)   64
   Publishing to a Maven Repository   64
   Maven2Gradle Build Script Converter   66
   Maven POM Import   67
   Conclusion   69

5. **Testing with Gradle** **71**
   JUnit   71
   TestNG   74
   Spock   75
   Geb and EasyB   76
   Gradle's Testing Focus   79

6. **Multiproject Builds** **81**
   Multiproject Build Structure   81
   Project-Specific Build Files   82
   One Master Build File   85
   A Hybrid Multiproject Build   86
   Individual, Unified, or Hybrid?   87

Multiproject Task Structure   88
Multiple Projects Your Way   89

Foreword

It is a great pleasure to have this first book of the Gradle O'Reilly series in my virtual hands. There could be no better endorsement of Gradle as a technology than to have such outstanding technologists as Tim and Matthew to think it worthwhile to write a book series on the subject.

In our experience, automation—not mere building—is a crucial part of shipping software successfully. We are very happy that more and more organizations are choosing Gradle as their tool of choice for modeling and choreographing their automation needs.

This book is the best available introduction into Gradle. It is wonderfully written. The presentation of the topics reflect the extraordinary teaching skills of the authors. The book provides an excellent start and orientation for the Gradle technology.

—Hans Dockter, Founder of Gradle and CEO of Gradleware

Preface

Introduction

This book has a very clear aim: introduce you to the incredible simplicity and power of Gradle.

Gradle is a flexible yet model-driven JVM-based build tool. Gradle acknowledges and improves on the very best ideas from Make, Ant, Ivy, Maven, Rake, Gant, Scons, SBT, Leinengen, and Buildr. The best-of-breed features previously scattered among a set of tools are now made available via a unified Groovy DSL for scripting and Java API for tooling. Gradle, even at the 1.0 milestone release current as of the time of this writing, already has a passionate following among some of the most respected enterprises and open source communities.

As we explore the tool's capabilities, you'll discover that Gradle is being heralded as more than just a build tool but also as a means of automating the compilation, test, and release process. In this first official book on this open source project, we'll showcase why the excitement around Gradle is on the rise and how it meets the challenge of these lofty build automation goals. Future volumes will cover the Gradle plug-in ecosystem, how to extend Gradle with your own build logic, and even more advanced topics. We're excited to have you along for the ride.

Tim Berglund and Matthew McCullough

Conventions Used in This Book

The following typographical conventions are used in this book:

Italic
> Indicates new terms, URLs, email addresses, filenames, and file extensions.

`Constant width`
> Used for program listings, as well as within paragraphs to refer to program elements such as variable or function names, databases, data types, environment variables, statements, and keywords.

`Constant width bold`
> Shows commands or other text that should be typed literally by the user.

`Constant width italic`
> Shows text that should be replaced with user-supplied values or by values determined by context.

> This icon signifies a tip, suggestion, or general note.

> This icon indicates a warning or caution.

Using Code Examples

This book is here to help you get your job done. In general, you may use the code in this book in your programs and documentation. You do not need to contact us for permission unless you're reproducing a significant portion of the code. For example, writing a program that uses several chunks of code from this book does not require permission. Selling or distributing a CD-ROM of examples from O'Reilly books does require permission. Answering a question by citing this book and quoting example code does not require permission. Incorporating a significant amount of example code from this book into your product's documentation does require permission.

All the code samples used in this book in addition to many others that supplement this learning effort can be found, fully open sourced, at *https://github.com/gradleware/oreilly-gradle-book-examples*

We appreciate, but do not require, attribution. An attribution usually includes the title, author, publisher, and ISBN. For example: "*Building and Testing with Gradle* by Tim Berglund and Matthew McCullough (O'Reilly). Copyright 2011 Gradle, Inc., 978-1-449-30463-8."

If you feel your use of code examples falls outside fair use or the permission given above, feel free to contact us at *permissions@oreilly.com*.

Safari® Books Online

Safari. Safari Books Online is an on-demand digital library that lets you easily search over 7,500 technology and creative reference books and videos to find the answers you need quickly.

With a subscription, you can read any page and watch any video from our library online. Read books on your cell phone and mobile devices. Access new titles before they are available for print, and get exclusive access to manuscripts in development and post feedback for the authors. Copy and paste code samples, organize your favorites, download chapters, bookmark key sections, create notes, print out pages, and benefit from tons of other time-saving features.

O'Reilly Media has uploaded this book to the Safari Books Online service. To have full digital access to this book and others on similar topics from O'Reilly and other publishers, sign up for free at *http://my.safaribooksonline.com*.

How to Contact Us

Please address comments and questions concerning this book to the publisher:

O'Reilly Media, Inc.
1005 Gravenstein Highway North
Sebastopol, CA 95472
800-998-9938 (in the United States or Canada)
707-829-0515 (international or local)
707-829-0104 (fax)

We have a web page for this book, where we list errata, examples, and any additional information. You can access this page at:

http://www.oreilly.com/catalog/0636920019909

To comment or ask technical questions about this book, send email to:

bookquestions@oreilly.com

For more information about our books, courses, conferences, and news, see our website at *http://www.oreilly.com*.

Find us on Facebook: *http://facebook.com/oreilly*

Follow us on Twitter: *http://twitter.com/oreillymedia*

Watch us on YouTube: *http://www.youtube.com/oreillymedia*

Acknowledgments from Tim Berglund

I'm delighted to be a part of this, the first book on Gradle to be available to the marketplace. It's not every day that a game-changing technology comes along, and it's exciting to be a small part of one when it does. Gradle is just such an opportunity for everyone reading this book.

Writing a book is enormously difficult work, even when it's a small one and you share the load with a coauthor. I should start by thanking that coauthor, Matthew McCullough, for his organization, motivation, willingness to hold me accoutable, and of course his excellent contributions to this volume.

I would also like to thank Hans Dockter, Ken Sipe, Adam Murdoch, Peter Niederwieser, Szczepan Faber, and Luke Daley of the Gradleware team for their support in answering questions and providing feedback during the writing process. The technical accuracy of this volume would be dramatically compromised without them.

Thanks to Mike Loukides for his confidence in Gradle as a technology and his help in publishing this book under O'Reilly's name. Thanks also for the editorial contributions of Meghan Blanchette and Jasmine Perez.

The book also would not have been possible without the support of Jay Zimmerman of the No Fluff Just Stuff conference series. In five years, when Gradle has brought peace and order to all of your builds in ways you never could have anticipated, and you look back and realize you learned it all from these books, send Jay an email to say thanks. He won't know why you're sending it, but you will.

Finally, I want to thank my wife, Kari. I could have been called to other kinds of work which would have imposed less of a burden on her and conformed better to the assumptions she once made about what it is her husband would do, but instead she got this. Nevertheless, she believes in me and supports me in my vocation, including things like the writing of this book. These things likely would not happen if she hadn't.

The project of explaining Gradle continues, and these acknowledgments will follow it in the future volumes.

Acknowledgments from Matthew McCullough

Rich Remington for his detailed book review and edits.

Ken Sipe for his structural suggestions and content review.

Chris Beams for his legitimizing of Gradle through SpringSource projects.

Hans Dockter for his edits, but equally for his coinvention of this incredible new tool and belief that it can be stretched even further.

Adam Murdoch for his coinvention and equally meaningful technical edits of the book.

Tim Berglund for his sharing of the effort on authoring this book.

Jay Zimmerman for his encouragement and multifacted support of this technological and educational endeavor we call Gradle.

CHAPTER 1

Hello, Gradle!

Ant and Maven have occupied opposing positions on the build continuum, to the benefit and detriment of their users over the past decade. Ant chooses to offer extreme flexibility to the user, imposing no conventions whatsoever, and not wanting to impose any heavyweight dependency management infrastructure on the build. Apache Ivy later added badly needed dependency management to Java builds, but still didn't address the lack of conventions inherent in Ant. Maven, on the other hand, offered rigid standards and support for dependency management, but its standards were often over-bearing, and deviating from them often proved more difficult than expected.

Ant and Maven have shared considerable success in the Java marketplace, despite important shortcomings in both tools. On the one hand, Gradle presents itself as a sensible middle ground between both extremes, offering thoughtful conventions for your build to follow, and making it easy for you to extend or redefine those conventions when you want to. Gradle provides out-of-the-box build conventions and at the same time realizes that no one set of standards can accurately reflect every build. Gradle therefore intends to be a means of developing organization- and project-specific build standards. It is best thought of not as a set of opinions on build standards, but as a toolkit for developing and extending those standards with a rich, descriptive language.

Gradle also gives you options in the way it handles build dependencies. If your project's idiom is to declare a few top-level dependencies by name and let your build tool determine what other libraries must be present to support your declared dependencies ("transitive dependency management"), Gradle will let you do that, interfacing with both Maven and Ivy repositories. If you want to download JAR files and manage dependencies by hand in a local project directory, Gradle will not penalize you in any way. Both approaches are first-class options. This flexibility is important in many cases, but especially when migrating builds to Gradle: regardless of the legacy build's opinions on dependency management, Gradle will not oppose them.

Gradle is rich in features, but is not such an opinionated framework that it will fight you when you want to do things your own way. It offers conventions to those who want them, flexibility to those who need it, and a toolkit for turning that flexibility into domain-specific build standards that you can write on your own. Apart from its nuanced position on the convention/configuration continuum, it offers no shortage of helpful, high-productivity features absent from other build tools. We will explore these together throughout the book.

Build Files in Groovy

A potentially complex build file demands an expressive format. XML was an easy choice for a build tool a decade ago, when it was a new technology, developers were enthusiastic about it, and no one yet knew the pain of reading it in large quantities. It seemed to be human-readable, and it was very easy to write code to parse it. However, a decade of experience has shown that large and complex XML files are only easy for machines to read, not for humans. Also, XML's strictly hierarchical structure limits the expressiveness of the format. It's easy to show nesting relationships in XML, but it's hard to express program flow and data access the way most common programming language idioms express them. Ultimately, XML is the wrong format for a build file.

Gradle expresses its build files in Groovy. Groovy is a dynamic language of the JVM, similar in many respects to Java, but with some important differences. Every Gradle build file is an executable Groovy script. As a beginning Gradle user, you don't even need to be aware that you're writing Groovy code, but as your needs become more sophisticated, the power of the Groovy language may become very important. Unlike the build file formats of Ant and Maven, Gradle's Groovy-based build files allow you to do general-purpose programming tasks in your build file. This relieves much of the frustration developers have faced in lacking control flow in Ant or being forced into plug-in development in Maven to accomplish nonstandard tasks.

Domain-Specific Build Languages

Every developer maintaining a complex build has wanted at some point to write just a little bit of code in the build file. Sometime you just need an iterator, and other times you'd like to express a moderately complex conditional without resorting to major build file surgery. But is the unlimited ability to code your way through a complex build a good thing? It might open broad new vistas of flexibility, but the result might ultimately be a catastrophe of maintainability. Since Gradle build files are Groovy scripts, Gradle gives you the option to break into scripting mode at any point in your build, but doing this to excess is generally not encouraged.

Instead, Gradle intends to present the user not with mere Groovy, but with a domain-specific language (DSL) tailored to the task of building code. A Gradle user could learn this language, not previously having known Groovy, and use Gradle effectively. This DSL describes the build using idioms appropriate to the task of building software, not necessarily to general-purpose programming. General-purpose coding is always available as a fallback, but Gradle gently nudges the user toward using the idioms of its DSL first, and coding second.

When the standard Gradle DSL doesn't have the language to describe what you want your build to do, you can extend the DSL through plug-ins. For example, Gradle out of the box contains the language needed to describe how to build Java code and create a WAR file from the output. However, it doesn't contain the language needed to run database migration scripts or deploy code to a set of cloud-based QA servers. Through Gradle plug-ins, you can add new task definitions, change the behavior of existing tasks, add new objects, and create new keywords to describe tasks that depart from the standard Gradle categories. Even through the simple mechanism of a custom Gradle task, you can introduce small pieces of build vocabulary, turning an otherwise undesirable chunk of imperative code into a clean declaration.

If you are coming from Maven, your understanding of a plug-in may be quite different from Gradle's plug-in concept. In Maven, a plug-in is a means of extending the tool with a particular, fine-grained action to be performed during your build, often associated with one or more phases in Maven's elaborate lifecycle model. In Gradle, a plug-in may provide configurable build actions by introducing one or more tasks, but it is fundamentally a means of extending the build DSL to include the domain encompassed by the plug-in.

Using and extending the Gradle DSL are usually preferable to writing code in your build file. While you are always free to solve problems in a locally optimized way by writing Groovy code inside your build, the most maintainable builds will eventually refactor this code into organized plug-ins that expose new build language idioms to the build files that use them. Thus you can express the activities of your build in a high-level, declarative language that is meaningful in your business and technology domain.

Getting Started

Gradle is easy to install. For all platforms, the procedure is as follows:

- Visit *http://gradle.org/downloads.html* and download the current release
- Unzip the downloaded file into a directory of your choosing
- Add the environment variable `GRADLE_HOME`, pointing to the install directory (this is optional, but it makes the next step easier)
- Add `$GRADLE_HOME/bin` to your path

MacOS Installation with Brew

Gradle is maintained in the community-supported MacOS package manager, Homebrew (*http://mxcl.github.com/homebrew*), or "brew" for short. To install Gradle using brew, simply type the following from a Terminal window:

```
$ sudo brew install gradle
```

Brew will install and build any dependencies, then place the Gradle executable in your path.

Linux and MacOS Installation

To install Gradle on *nix operating systems like Linux and MacOS, follow this command-line script:

```
$ wget http://repo.gradle.org/gradle/distributions/gradle-1.0-bin.zip
--2011-03-18 10:58:46--  http://repo.gradle.org/gradle/distributions/
gradle-1.0-bin.zip
Resolving repo.gradle.org... 50.16.203.43
Connecting to gradle.artifactoryonline.com |50.16.203.43|:80... connected.
HTTP request sent, awaiting response... 200 OK
Length: 26899590 (26M) [application/zip]
Saving to: `gradle-1.0-bin.zip'

100%[=============================================================>]
26,899,590    171K/s   in 2m 56s

2011-03-18 11:01:42 (149 KB/s) - `gradle-1.0-bin.zip' saved [26899590/26899590]

$ sudo unzip -q gradle-1.0-bin.zip -d /usr/local/
$ echo "export GRADLE_HOME=/usr/local/gradle-1.0" >> .profile
$ echo "export PATH=$PATH:$GRADLE_HOME/bin" >> .profile
```

 You can also download the Gradle distribution directly from the Gradle web site (*http://gradle.org/downloads.html*) and unzip that file. Also, you may prefer another mechanism of setting environment variables on your installation. Feel free to use whatever works for you.

Windows Installation

To install Gradle on Windows, do the following:

- Download the Gradle ZIP file from the Gradle web site (*http://gradle.org/downloads .html*) and double-click on it to unzip. Drag the folder to a location of your choosing. In this example, we'll assume you put it in *C:\gradle-1.0*.

- Next, right-click on the My Computer icon and select Properties.

- In the System Control Panel window, select Advanced System Settings from the links on the left.
- In the Advanced System Settings dialog box (Figure 1-1), click on the Environment Variables button.

Figure 1-1. Windows Advanced System Settings dialog

 The screenshots shown here are taken from Windows 7 SP1. Your version of Windows may vary.

- In the Environment Variables dialog box, click the New button under System Variables (Figure 1-2). Name the environment variable GRADLE_HOME, and give it the value C:\gradle-1.0. (If you unzipped Gradle into a different directory, put that directory here.)

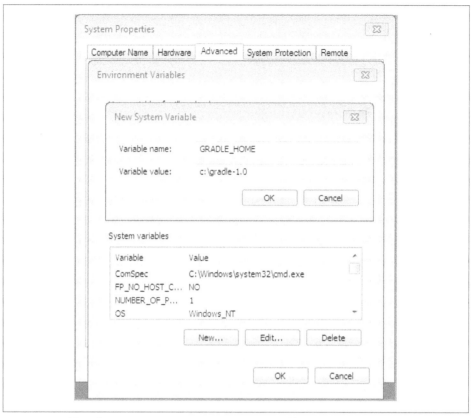

Figure 1-2. Adding the GRADLE_HOME environment variable

- In that same dialog box, select the Path variable under System Variables (Figure 1-3), then click Edit. Add the text `;%GRADLE_HOME%\bin` to the end of the Path variable value.

The Hello World Build File

Now that we have Gradle installed, we can start using it. Let's build the simplest build file that we possibly can to get an idea of the basics.

 Unless otherwise noted, all of the examples in this book will assume that you are running Gradle from the command line. See the installation procedures in "Getting Started" on page 3 for help getting started.

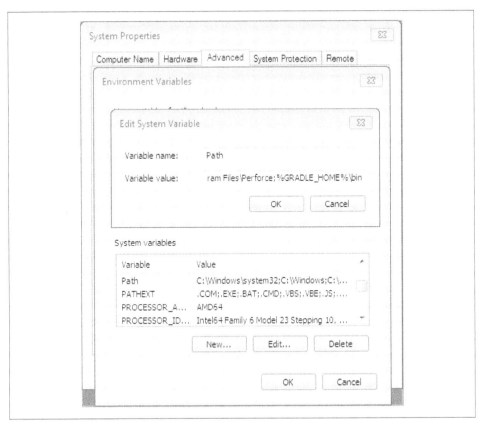

Figure 1-3. Editing the path

Create a file called `build.gradle` that looks like Example 1-1.

Example 1-1. Hello World build file

```
task helloWorld << {
  println 'hello, world'
}
```

You will see the following output as a result of the *Hello World* build:

```
$ gradle -q helloWorld
hello, world
```

Note that the build file isn't required to include anything, and doesn't rely on any external dependencies. It also doesn't do much, other than printing out a message. Before we move on to building some Java code, let's try one more example. This time, we'll use two tasks plus a dependency to get the same work done (Example 1-2).

Example 1-2. Hello World in two tasks

```
task hello << {
  print 'hello, '
}

task world(dependsOn: hello) << {
  println 'world'
}
```

To run this build, we execute the second task, `world`. It produces remarkably similar output to the first:

```
$ gradle -q world
hello, world
```

Building a Java Program

Of course, the Hello World example is contrived; nobody really wants to execute a build that only prints messages to the console. Let's have a look at how easy it can be to build Java code. In the spirit of this introduction, we'll make it a very simple Java program, just to showcase how simple Gradle can make a build if you are comfortable following its conventions.

The build file looks as shown in Example 1-3.

Example 1-3. The Simplest Possible Gradle Build File for Java

```
apply plugin: 'java'
```

The source code looks as shown in Example 1-4.

Example 1-4. Hello World in Java

```
package org.gradle.example.simple;

public class HelloWorld {
    public static void main(String args[]) {
        System.out.println("hello, world");
    }
}
```

Importantly, the directory layout of the project looks as shown in Example 1-5.

Example 1-5. Project layout of Hello World Java

```
.
├── build.gradle
    └── src
        └── main
            └── java
                └── org
                    └── gradle
                        └── example
```

```
            └── simple
                └── HelloWorld.java
```

This build file automatically introduces a number of tasks for us to run. Just run `gradle build`, and you'll see the output shown in Example 1-6.

Example 1-6. Project Layout of Hello World Java After Build

```
.
├── build
│   ├── classes
│   │   └── main
│   │       └── org
│   │           └── gradle
│   │               └── example
│   │                   └── simple
│   │                       └── HelloWorld.class
│   ├── dependency-cache
│   ├── libs
│   │   └── minimal-java-build-file.jar
│   ├── reports
│   │   └── tests
│   │       ├── css3-pie-1.0beta3.htc
│   │       ├── index.html
│   │       ├── report.js
│   │       └── style.css
│   └── test-results
├── build.gradle
├── run-example.bsh
└── src
    └── main
        └── java
            └── org
                └── gradle
                    └── example
                        └── simple
                            └── HelloWorld.java
```

Notice not only that the Java code has been compiled and its class file placed in a directory we didn't have to configure, but also that test report files have been generated (ready to receive actual unit test results when we write tests later), and a JAR has been built using the project directory name as the filename. This is all a result of the conventions of Gradle's Java plug-in. We didn't have to make a single decision or write a line of configuration. And let it not go without saying that we can run our nascent Java application as shown in Example 1-7.

Example 1-7. Running Hello World Java

```
$ java -cp build/classes/main/ org.gradle.example.simple.HelloWorld
hello, world
```

There is a much longer story to tell about the Java plug-in, which will be covered in a separate volume. If you want to get started now, you should also check out the online documentation (*http://www.gradle.org/current/docs/userguide/userguide.html*).

 If you had to write a real-world build file to build and run a Java program, you would want to use the application plug-in, which is a core plug-in available with every installation of Gradle.

The Gradle Command Line

The preceding examples have shown Gradle running from the command line, and the majority of this book will continue that pattern. Gradle is designed to support first-class IDE integration at a deep architectural level, but the command line is anything but a second-class citizen. In this book, we will work primarily from the command line.

We won't go over all possible command line options, but here's what you need to be productive right away:

--help *or* -h
  Prints out the help messages describing all command-line options.

-Dproperty=value
  Defines a system property. This is a useful mechanism for passing parameters into a build from the command line. Example: -Dcustom.config=my-config.properties.

--info *or* -i
  Sets the Gradle log level to INFO, which causes a few more informative messages to be emitted over the default setting.

--debug *or* -d
  Turns out debug logging for the build, including stack traces. This generates a lot of output, but can be quite useful for troubleshooting build problems.

--dry-run *or* -m
  Evaluates and runs the build file, but does not execute any task actions.

--quiet *or* -q
  Suppresses most output, showing error messages only.

--gui
  Launches the Gradle GUI.

--stacktrace *or* -s
  Emits an abbreviated stack trace when an exception is thrown by the build. Normally, stack trace logging is suppressed, so this is a helpful switch when debugging a broken build. The stack trace is abbreviated by removing frames related to purely internal Groovy method calls.

--full-stacktrace *or* -S
> Emits a longer version of the --stacktrace output, including all internal Groovy method calls. These are usually not of interest to the build developer.

properties
> Emits all the properties of the build's Project object. The Project object is an object representing the structure and state of the current build.

tasks
> Emits a list of all tasks available in the current build file. Note that plug-ins may introduce tasks of their own, so this list may be longer than the tasks you have defined.

CHAPTER 2

Gradle Tasks

Inside of a Gradle build file, the fundamental unit of build activity is the task. Tasks are named collections of build instructions that Gradle executes as it performs a build. You've already seen examples of tasks in Chapter 1, and they may seem like a familiar abstraction compared to other build systems, but Gradle provides a richer model than you may be used to. Rather than bare declarations of build activity tied together with dependencies, Gradle tasks are first-class objects available to you to program if you desire.

Let's take a look at the different ways of defining a task, the two key aspects of task definitions, and the task API we can use to perform our own customization.

Declaring a Task

In the introduction, we saw how to create a task and assign it behavior all at the same time. However, there's an even simpler way to create a task. All you need is a task name (Example 2-1).

Example 2-1. Declaring a task by name only

```
task hello
```

You can see the results of this by running **gradle tasks** (Example 2-2).

Example 2-2. Gradle's report of the newly created task

```
------------------------------------------------------------
Root Project
------------------------------------------------------------

Help tasks
----------
dependencies - Displays the dependencies of root project 'task-lab'.
help - Displays a help message
projects - Displays the subprojects of root project 'task-lab'.
properties - Displays the properties of root project 'task-lab'.
```

```
tasks - Displays the tasks in root project 'task-lab'.

Other tasks
-----------
hello
```

Task Action

However, executing this task with `gradle hello` will not produce any result, because we haven't yet assigned the task an action. Previously, we assigned an action to a task with the left-shift operator (Example 2-3).

Example 2-3. Giving a task a trivial action to perform

```
task hello << {
  println 'hello, world'
}
```

 In Groovy, operators like << (the "left-shift" operator from Java) can be overloaded to have different meanings depending upon the types of the objects they operate on. In this case, Gradle has overloaded << to append a code block to the list of actions a task performs. This is equivalent to the doLast() method we'll cover later in the chapter.

However, we now have the flexibility of accruing action code in the task by referring to the task object we've created (Example 2-4).

Example 2-4. Appending a task's actions one at a time

```
task hello

hello << {
  print 'hello, '
}

hello << {
  println 'world'
}
```

Now we can recover our familiar build output (Example 2-5).

Example 2-5. The output of the build with actions appended a piece at a time

```
$ gradle hello
hello, world
$
```

This is again trivial build behavior, but it exposes a powerful insight: tasks are not one-off declarations of build activity, but are first-class objects in the Gradle programming environment. And if we can accrue build actions to them over the course of the build file, there's probably more we can do. Let's keep exploring.

Task Configuration

New users of Gradle commonly stumble over the configuration syntax when trying to define task actions. Continuing our previous example, we can expand it to include a configuration block (Example 2-6).

Example 2-6. A mix of task configuration and task action definition

```
task initializeDatabase
initializeDatabase << { println 'connect to database' }
initializeDatabase << { println 'update database schema' }
initializeDatabase { println 'configuring database connection' }
```

Running this build file, we get what may seem to be a counterintuitive result (Example 2-7).

Example 2-7. The output of the preceding build file

```
$ gradle -b scratch.gradle initializeDatabase
configuring database connection
:initializeDatabase
connect to database
update database schema
$
```

 Groovy uses the term "closure" to refer to a block of code between two curly braces. A closure functions like an object that can be passed as a parameter to a method or assigned to a variable, then executed later. You'll see closures all over in Gradle, since they're a perfect fit for holding blocks of configuration code and build actions.

If the third closure had been just another snippet of build action, then we'd expect its message to print last, not first. It turns out that the closure added to the task name *without* the left-shift operator doesn't create additional task action code at all. Instead, it is a *configuration* block. The configuration block of a task is run during Gradle's *configuration* lifecycle phase, which runs before the *execution* phase, when task actions are executed.

Every time Gradle executes a build, it runs through three lifecycle phases: initialization, configuration, and execution. Execution is the phase in which build tasks are executed in the order required by their dependency relationships. Configuration is the phase in which those task objects are assembled into an internal object model, usually called the DAG (for *directed acyclic graph*). Initialization is the phase in which Gradle decides which projects are to participate in the build. The latter phase is important in multiproject builds.

Configuration closures are additive just like action closures, so we could have written the previous build file like so, and we would see the same output (Example 2-8).

Example 2-8. Appending configuration blocks

```
task initializeDatabase
initializeDatabase << { println 'connect to database' }
initializeDatabase << { println 'update database schema' }
initializeDatabase { print 'configuring ' }
initializeDatabase { println 'database connection' }
```

The configuration block is the place to set up variables and data structures that will be needed by the task action when (and if) it runs later on in the build. The configuration structure gives you the opportunity to turn your build's tasks into a rich object model populated with information about the build, rather than a mere set of build actions to be executed in some sequence. Without this distinction between configuration and action, you'd have to build additional complexity into your task dependency relationships, resulting in a more fragile build and a much less expressive means of communicating the build's essential data structures.

 All build configuration code runs every time you run a Gradle build file, regardless of whether any given task runs during execution.

Tasks Are Objects

It may have occurred to you by now that Gradle is creating an internal object model of your build before executing it. This is, in fact, explicitly what Gradle is doing. Every task you declare is actually a task object contained within the overall project. A task object has properties and methods just like any other object. We can even control the type of each task object, and access unique, type-specific functionality accordingly. A few examples will help make this clear.

By default, each new task receives the type of `DefaultTask`. Like `java.lang.Object` in Java code, every Gradle task descends from this object type—even tasks that extend the `DefaultTask` type with a type of their own. DefaultTasks don't actually *do* anything like compile code or copy files, but they do contain the functionality required for them to interface with the Gradle project model. Let's take a look at the methods and properties each and every Gradle task has.

Methods of DefaultTask

dependsOn(task)

Adds a task as a dependency of the calling task. A depended-on task will always run before the task that depends on it. There are several ways to invoke this method. If task world depends on task hello, we could use the code shown in Example 2-9.

Example 2-9. Different ways of calling the dependsOn method

```
// Declare that world depends on hello
// Preserves any previously defined dependencies as well
task loadTestData {
  dependsOn createSchema
}

// An alternate way to express the same dependency
task loadTestData {
  dependsOn << createSchema
}

// Do the same using single quotes (which are usually optional)
task loadTestData {
  dependsOn 'createSchema'
}

// Explicitly call the method on the task object
task loadTestData
loadTestData.dependsOn createSchema

// A shortcut for declaring dependencies
task loadTestData(dependsOn: createSchema)
```

A task can depend on more than one task. If task loadTestData depends on tasks createSchema and compileTestClasses, we could use the code shown in Example 2-10.

Example 2-10. Different ways of calling the dependsOn method for multiple dependencies

```
// Declare dependencies one at a time
task loadTestData {
  dependsOn << compileTestClasses
  dependsOn << createSchema
}

// Pass dependencies as a variable-length list
task world {
  dependsOn compileTestClasses, createSchema
}
```

```
// Explicitly call the method on the task object
task world
world.dependsOn compileTestClasses, createSchema

// A shortcut for dependencies only
// Note the Groovy list syntax
task world(dependsOn: [ compileTestClasses, createSchema ])
```

doFirst(closure)

Adds a block of executable code to the beginning of a task's action. During the execution phase, the action block of every relevant task is executed. The `doFirst` method allows you to add a bit of behavior to the beginning of an existing action, even if that action is defined by a build file or a plug-in you don't control. Calling `doFirst` multiple times keeps appending new blocks of action code to the beginning of the task's execution sequence.

You can invoke the `doFirst` method directly on the task object, passing a closure to the method. The closure contains the code to run before the task's existing action.

 As we've already mentioned, a closure is a block of Groovy code inside a pair of curly braces. You can pass a closure around just like any other object. Passing closures to methods is a common Groovy idiom.

Example 2-11. Calling the doFirst method on the task object

```
task setupDatabaseTests << {
  // This is the task's existing action
  println 'load test data'
}

setupDatabaseTests.doFirst {
  println 'create schema'
}
```

Example 2-12. The results of the preceding build file

```
$ gradle setupDatabaseTests
:setupDatabaseTests
create schema
load test data
$
```

You can also invoke `doFirst` from within the task's configuration block. Recall that the configuration block is a piece of executable code that runs before any task's action runs, during the configuration phase of the build. In our earlier discussion of task configuration, you may have been wondering how you might practically use the configuration block. This example shows how you can call task methods from inside the configuration block, which makes a potentially very expressive format for modifying task behavior (Example 2-13).

Example 2-13. Calling the doFirst method inside the task's configuration block

```
task setupDatabaseTests << {
  println 'load test data'
}

setupDatabaseTests {
  doFirst {
    println 'create schema'
  }
}
```

Repeated calls to the doFirst method are additive. Each previous call's action code is retained, and the new closure is appended to the start of the list to be executed in order. If we had to set up a database for integration testing (and wanted to do it a piece at a time), we might use the code shown in Example 2-14.

Example 2-14. Repeated calls to doFirst are cumulative

```
task setupDatabaseTests << {
  println 'load test data'
}

setupDatabaseTests.doFirst {
  println 'create database schema'
}

setupDatabaseTests.doFirst {
  println 'drop database schema'
}
```

Example 2-15. The output of the preceding example

```
$ gradle world
:setupDatabaseTests
drop database schema
create database schema
load test data
$
```

Of course, it's somewhat contrived to break one initialization sequence into three separate closures and calls to doFirst(), as we've done here. However, sometimes the initial definition of a task isn't immediately available to change as you see fit—for example, in cases in which the task is defined in another build file that is impossible or impractical for you to modify. This kind of programmatic modification of that otherwise inaccessible build logic can be very powerful.

So far, our examples have used a very simple syntax, which makes the mechanics of Gradle more obvious, though at the expense of a lot of repetition. In a real-world build (still relying on println statements in place of actual testing actions), we would be more likely to structure the task as done in Example 2-16.

Example 2-16. Repeated calls to doFirst, refactored

```
// Initial task definition (maybe not easily editable)
task setupDatabaseTests << {
  println 'load test data'
}

// Our changes to the task (in a place we can edit them)
setupDatabaseTests {
  doFirst {
    println 'create database schema'
  }
  doFirst {
    println 'drop database schema'
  }
}
```

Note that we gather together the multiple calls to doFirst inside a single configuration block, and this occurs after the initial action is added to the world task.

doLast(closure)

The doLast method is very similar to the doFirst() method, except that it appends behavior to the end of an action, rather than before it. If there was a block of code you wanted to run after an existing task was done executing, you might do as shown in Example 2-17:

Example 2-17. An example of the doLast method

```
task setupDatabaseTests << {
  println 'create database schema'
}

setupDatabaseTests.doLast {
  println 'load test data'
}
```

Just like doFirst, repeated calls to doLast are additive. Each succeeding call appends its closure to the end of the list to be executed in order (Example 2-18).

Example 2-18. Repeated calls to doLast are additive

```
task setupDatabaseTests << {
  println 'create database schema'
}

setupDatabaseTests.doLast {
  println 'load test data'
}

setupDatabaseTests.doLast {
  println 'update version table'
}
```

As discussed in "Task Action" on page 14, the << operator is another way of expressing a call to the doLast() method.

onlyIf(closure)

The onlyIf method allows you to express a predicate which determines whether a task should be executed. The value of the predicate is the value returned by the closure. Using this method, you can disable the execution of a task which might otherwise run as a normal part of the build's dependency chain.

 In Groovy, the last statement of a closure is the closure's return value, even if no return statement is given. A Groovy method containing a single expression is a function that returns the value of that expression.

Example 2-19. A build file making use of the onlyIf method.

```
task createSchema << {
  println 'create database schema'
}

task loadTestData(dependsOn: createSchema) << {
  println 'load test data'
}

loadTestData.onlyIf {
  System.properties['load.data'] == 'true'
}
```

Example 2-20. Two invocations of the preceding build file. Note differing results.

```
$ build loadTestData

create database schema
:loadTestData SKIPPED

$ gradle -Dload.data=true loadTestData
:createSchema
create database schema
:loadTestData
load test data
$
```

Using the onlyIf method, you can switch individual tasks on and off using any logic you can express in Groovy code, not just the simple System property tests we've used here. You can read files, call web services, check security credentials, or just about anything else.

Properties of DefaultTask

didWork

A boolean property indicating whether the task completed successfully. Not all tasks may set `didWork` upon completion, but some built-in tasks like `Compile`, `Copy`, and `Delete` do set it to reflect the success or failure of their actions. The evaluation of a task having worked is task-specific. For example, the current implementation of the `Java Compiler` returns `didWork` of true if at least one file successfully compiled. You are able to set the `didWork` property in your own task actions to reflect the results of build code you write.

Example 2-21. Send an email upon successful compilation

```
apply plugin: 'java'

task emailMe(dependsOn: compileJava) << {
  if(tasks.compileJava.didWork) {
    println 'SEND EMAIL ANNOUNCING SUCCESS'
  }
}
```

Example 2-22. The results of the didWork build

```
$ gradle -b didWork.gradle emailMe
SEND EMAIL ANNOUNCING SUCCESS
$
```

enabled

A boolean property indicating whether the task will execute. You can set any task's `enabled` property to false to cause it not to run. Its dependencies will still execute the way they would if the task were enabled.

Example 2-23. Disabling a task

```
task templates << {
  println 'process email templates'
}

task sendEmails(dependsOn: templates) << {
  println 'send emails'
}

sendEmails.enabled = false
```

Example 2-24. The build with a task disabled. Note that the dependency still runs.

```
$ gradle -b enabled.gradle sendEmails
:templates
process email templates
:sendEmails SKIPPED
$
```

The -b command line switch points Gradle to a nondefault build file. By default, it looks for a file called `build.gradle`, but this switch lets us point it at a different file.

path

A string property containing the fully qualified path of a task. By default, a task's path is simply the name of the task with a leading colon. The following build file illustrates this.

Example 2-25. A single-level build file that echoes its only task's path

```
task echoMyPath << {
  println "THIS TASK'S PATH IS ${path}"
}
```

Example 2-26. The results of the previous build file

```
$ gradle -b path.gradle echoMyPath
THIS TASK'S PATH IS :echoMyPath
$
```

The leading colon indicates that the task is located in the top-level build file. However, for a given build, not all tasks must be present in the top-level build file, since Gradle supports dependent subprojects, or nested builds. If the task existed in a nested build called `subProject`, then the path would be `:subProject:echoMyPath`. For more details on nested builds, see Chapter 6.

logger

A reference to the internal Gradle `logger` object. The Gradle `logger` implements the org.slf4j.Logger interface, but with a few extra logging levels added. The logging levels supported by the `logger` are as follows. Setting the log level to one enables log output from all succeeding log levels, with the exception of `WARN` and `QUIET` as noted:

- `DEBUG`. For high-volume logging messages which are of interest to the build developer, but should be suppressed during normal build execution. When this log level is selected, Gradle automatically provides a richer log formatter, including the timestamp, log level, and logger name of each message. All other log levels emit only the undecorated log message.
- `INFO`. For lower-volume informative build messages which may be of optional interest during build execution.
- `LIFECYCLE`. Low-volume messages, usually from Gradle itself, about changes in the build lifecycle and the execution of the build tool. When Gradle is executed without the -q command line option, this is the default logging level. Calls to the `println` method emit log statements at this level.

- **WARN.** Low-volume but important messages, alerting the executor of the build of potential problems. When the log level is set to WARN, QUIET-level messages are not emitted.

- **QUIET.** Messages which should appear even if the quiet switch was specified on the Gradle command line. (Executing Gradle with the -q command line option causes this to be the default log level.) System.out.println is directed to the logger at this log level. When the log level is set to QUIET, WARN-level messages are not emitted.

- **ERROR.** Rare but critically important log messages which should be emitted in all cases. Intended to communicate build failures. If the log level is set to ERROR, calls to System.out.println will not show up in the console.

Example 2-27. A task illustrating the effects of each logging level. This slightly trickier Groovy code sets the log level to each of the valid options, attempting to emit a log message at each log level each time.

```
task logLevel << {
  def levels = ['DEBUG',
                'INFO',
                'LIFECYCLE',
                'QUIET',
                'WARN',
                'ERROR']
  levels.each { level ->
    logging.level = level
    def logMessage = "SETTING LogLevel=${level}"
    logger.error logMessage
    logger.error '-' * logMessage.size()
    logger.debug 'DEBUG ENABLED'
    logger.info 'INFO ENABLED'
    logger.lifecycle 'LIFECYCLE ENABLED'
    logger.warn 'WARN ENABLED'
    logger.quiet 'QUIET ENABLED'
    logger.error 'ERROR ENABLED'
    println 'THIS IS println OUTPUT'
    logger.error ' '
  }
}
```

Example 2-28. The output generated by the preceding build file.

```
$ gradle -b logging.gradle logLevel
 16:02:34.883 [ERROR] [org.gradle.api.Task] SETTING LogLevel=DEBUG
 16:02:34.902 [ERROR] [org.gradle.api.Task] ----------------------
 16:02:34.903 [DEBUG] [org.gradle.api.Task] DEBUG ENABLED
 16:02:34.903 [INFO] [org.gradle.api.Task] INFO ENABLED
 16:02:34.904 [LIFECYCLE] [org.gradle.api.Task] LIFECYCLE ENABLED
 16:02:34.904 [WARN] [org.gradle.api.Task] WARN ENABLED
 16:02:34.905 [QUIET] [org.gradle.api.Task] QUIET ENABLED
 16:02:34.905 [ERROR] [org.gradle.api.Task] ERROR ENABLED
 16:02:34.906 [ERROR] [org.gradle.api.Task]
 SETTING LogLevel=INFO
 --------------------
```

```
INFO ENABLED
LIFECYCLE ENABLED
WARN ENABLED
QUIET ENABLED
ERROR ENABLED

SETTING LogLevel=LIFECYCLE
--------------------------
LIFECYCLE ENABLED
WARN ENABLED
QUIET ENABLED
ERROR ENABLED

SETTING LogLevel=QUIET
----------------------
QUIET ENABLED
ERROR ENABLED

SETTING LogLevel=WARN
---------------------
WARN ENABLED
ERROR ENABLED

SETTING LogLevel=ERROR
----------------------
ERROR ENABLED
$
```

logging

The `logging` property gives us access to the log level. As illustrated in the discussion of the logger property, the `logging.level` property can be read and written to change the logging level in use by the build.

description

The `description` property is just what it sounds like: a small piece of human-readable metadata to document the purpose of a task. There are several ways of setting a description, as shown in Example 2-29 and Example 2-30.

Example 2-29. Setting the description and task behavior all in one

```
task helloWorld(description: 'Says hello to the world') << {
  println 'hello, world'
}
```

Example 2-30. The two ways of declaring task behavior and description separately

```
task helloWorld << {
  println 'hello, world'
}

helloWorld {
  description = 'Says hello to the world'
```

```
}

// Another way to do it
helloWorld.description = 'Says hello to the world'
```

temporaryDir

The `temporaryDir` property returns a `File` object pointing to a temporary directory belonging to this build file. This directory is generally available to a task needing a temporary place in which to store intermediate results of any work, or to stage files for processing inside the task.

Dynamic Properties

As we've seen, tasks come with a set of intrinsic properties which are indispensable to the Gradle user. However, we can also assign any other properties we want to a task. A task object functions like a hash map, able to contain whatever other arbitrary property names and values we care to assign to it (as long as the names don't collide with the built-in property names).

Leaving our familiar "hello, world" example, let's suppose we had a task called `createArtifact` that depended on a task called `copyFiles`. The job of the `copyFiles` is to collect files from several sources and copy them into a staging directory, which the `createArtifact` task will later assemble into a deployment artifact. The list of files may change depending on the parameters of the build, but the artifact must contain a manifest listing them, to satisfy some requirement of the deployed application. This is a perfect occasion to use a dynamic property (Example 2-31 and Example 2-32).

Example 2-31. Build file showing a dynamic task property

```
task copyFiles {
  // Find files from wherever, copy them
  // (then hardcode a list of files for illustration)
  fileManifest = [ 'data.csv', 'config.json' ]
}

task createArtifact(dependsOn: copyFiles) << {
  println "FILES IN MANIFEST: ${copyFiles.fileManifest}"
}
```

Example 2-32. The output of the above build file

```
$ gradle -b dynamic.gradle createArtifact
 FILES IN MANIFEST: [data.csv, config.json]
$
```

Task Types

As we discussed in "Tasks Are Objects" on page 16, every task has a type. Besides the `DefaultTask`, there are task types for copying, archiving, executing programs, and many more. Declaring a task type is a lot like extending a base class in an object-oriented programming language: you can get certain methods and properties available in your task for free. This makes for very concise task definitions that can accomplish a lot.

A complete task reference is beyond the scope of this volume, but here are a few important types with an example of how to use each.

Copy

A copy task copies files from one place into another (Example 2-33). In its most basic form, it copies files from one directory into another, with optional restrictions on which file patterns are included or excluded.

Example 2-33. A simple example of the copy task

```
task copyFiles(type: Copy) {
  from 'resources'
  into 'target'
  include '**/*.xml', '**/*.txt', '**/*.properties'
}
```

The copy task will create the destination directory if it doesn't already exist. In this case, the copyFiles task will copy any files with the .xml, .properties, or .txt extensions from the resources directory to the target directory. Note that the `from`, `into`, and `include` methods are inherited from the `Copy`.

Jar

A Jar task creates a Jar file from source files (Example 2-34). The Java plug-in creates a task of this type, called unsurprisingly `jar`. It packages the main source set and resources together with a trivial manifest into a Jar bearing the project's name in the `build/libs` directory. The task is highly customizable.

Example 2-34. A simple example of the Jar task in the jar-task example project

```
apply plugin: 'java'

task customJar(type: Jar) {
  manifest {
    attributes firstKey: 'firstValue', secondKey: 'secondValue'
  }
  archiveName = 'hello.jar'
  destinationDir = file("${buildDir}/jars")
  from sourceSets.main.classes
}
```

Note that the archive name and destination directory are easily configurable. Likewise, the manifest can be populated with custom attributes using a readable Groovy map syntax. The contents of the JAR are identified by the `from sourceSets.main.classes` line, which specifies that the compiled .class files of the main Java sources are to be included. The `from` method is identical to the one used in the `CopyTask` example, which reveals an interesting insight: the Jar task extends the Copy task. Even before we've seen exhaustive documentation of the Gradle object model and DSL, these details hint at the richness and order of the underlying structure.

The expression being assigned to `destinationDir` is worth noting. It would be natural just to assign a string to `destinationDir`, but the property expects an argument compatible with `java.io.File`. The `file()` method, which is always available inside a Gradle build file, converts the string to a `File` object.

 Remember, you can always open the `docs/dsl/index.html` file for documentation on standard Gradle features like the Jar task. Complete documentation of the Jar task and its companion tasks is beyond the scope of this book.

JavaExec

A JavaExec task runs a Java class with a main() method. Command-line Java can be a hassle, but this task tries to take the hassle away and integrate command-line Java invocations into your build.

Example 2-35. A Gradle task executing a command-line Java program (from the javaexec-task example)

```
apply plugin: 'java'

repositories {
  mavenCentral()
}

dependencies {
  runtime 'commons-codec:commons-codec:1.5'
}

task encode(type: JavaExec, dependsOn: classes) {
  main = 'org.gradle.example.commandline.MetaphoneEncoder'
  args = "The rain in Spain falls mainly in the plain".split().toList()
  classpath sourceSets.main.classesDir
  classpath configurations.runtime
}
```

The classpath property in the `encode` task is set to something called `configuration.runtime`. A configuration is a collection of dependencies that have something in common. In this case, the `runtime` configuration holds all dependencies which must be available to the program at runtime. This is in contrast to dependencies which are needed only during compilation, or only while tests are running, or which are needed at compile time and runtime, but which are provided by a runtime environment like an application server. The `configuration` property in Gradle is a collection of all configurations defined by the build, each of which is a collection of actual dependencies.

This build file declares an external dependency: the Apache Commons Codec library. Normally, we'd have to compile our Java file, then concoct a `java` command line including the path to the compiled class files and the JAR dependency. In this build file, however, we simply identify the main class to be run (`org.gradle.example.command line.MetaphoneEncoder`), provide it with some command line arguments in the form of a `List`, and point it at the Gradle classpath elements it needs. In this case, we may symbolically refer to the classes of the main sourceSet and all of the dependencies declared in the `compile` configuration. If we had a complex set of dozens of dependencies from multiple repositories—including even some statically managed dependencies in the project directory—this simple task would still work.

Custom Task Types

There will be occasions in which Gradle's built-in task types will not quite do the job, and instead, the most expressive way to develop your build will be to create a custom task. Gradle has several ways of doing this. We will discuss the two most common ways here.

Custom Tasks Types in the Build File

Suppose your build file needs to issue arbitrary queries against a MySQL database. There are several ways to accomplish this in Gradle, but you decide a custom task is the most expressive way to do it. The easiest way to introduce the task is simply to create it in your build script as shown here:

Example 2-36. A custom task to perform queries against a MySQL database (from the custom-task example)

```
task createDatabase(type: MySqlTask) {
  sql = 'CREATE DATABASE IF NOT EXISTS example'
}

task createUser(type: MySqlTask, dependsOn: createDatabase) {
  sql = "GRANT ALL PRIVILEGES ON example.*
  TO exampleuser@localhost IDENTIFIED BY 'passw0rd'"
```

```
}

task createTable(type: MySqlTask, dependsOn: createUser) {
  username = 'exampleuser'
  password = 'passw0rd'
  database = 'example'
  sql = 'CREATE TABLE IF NOT EXISTS users
  (id BIGINT PRIMARY KEY, username VARCHAR(100))'
}

class MySqlTask extends DefaultTask {
  def hostname = 'localhost'
  def port = 3306
  def sql
  def database
  def username = 'root'
  def password = 'password'

  @TaskAction
  def runQuery() {
    def cmd
    if(database) {
      cmd = "mysql -u ${username} -p${password} -h ${hostname}
      -P ${port} ${database} -e "
    }
    else {
      cmd = "mysql -u ${username} -p${password} -h ${hostname} -P ${port} -e "
    }
    project.exec {
      commandLine = cmd.split().toList() + sql
    }
  }
}
```

The custom task, MySqlTask, extends the DefaultTask class. All custom tasks must extend this class or one of its descendants. (A custom task can extend any task types other than DefaultTask. See Task Types for a description of the most important built-in task types.) The task declares properties (i.e., hostname, database, sql, etc.) in conventional Groovy idiom. It then declares a single method, runQuery(), which is annotated with the @TaskAction annotation. This method will run when the task runs.

The actual build tasks at the top of the build file all declare themselves to be of the MySqlTask type. By doing this, they automatically inherit the properties and action of that task class. Because most of the properties have defaults (some of which, like username and password, are obviously specific to the build), each invocation of the task has very little to configure. The createDatabase and createUser tasks are able to configure just a single SQL query, and allow the defaults to take over from there.

The createTable task overrides the username, password, and database properties, since its task dependencies have created a new database and username separate from the default administrative settings. The pattern of providing a useful default configuration which can be overridden when necessary is a recurring theme in Gradle.

Custom Tasks in the Source Tree

Significant custom task logic will not fit well into a build file. A few simple lines of scripting can pragmatically be inserted into a short task, as in the custom-task example. However, at some point, a sophisticated task will develop a class hierarchy of its own, might develop a reliance on external APIs, and will need automated testing. The build is code, and complex build code should be treated as a first-class citizen of the development world. Gradle makes this easy.

When custom task logic outgrows the build file, we can migrate it to the buildSrc directory at the project root. This directory is automatically compiled and added to the build classpath. Here is how we would alter the previous example to use the buildSrc directory.

Example 2-37. A build file using a custom task not defined in the build script

```
task createDatabase(type: MySqlTask) {
  sql = 'CREATE DATABASE IF NOT EXISTS example'
}

task createUser(type: MySqlTask, dependsOn: createDatabase) {
  sql = "GRANT ALL PRIVILEGES ON example.*
        TO exampleuser@localhost IDENTIFIED BY 'passw0rd'"
}

task createTable(type: MySqlTask, dependsOn: createUser) {
  username = 'exampleuser'
  password = 'passw0rd'
  database = 'example'
  sql = 'CREATE TABLE IF NOT EXISTS users
        (id BIGINT PRIMARY KEY, username VARCHAR(100))'
}
```

Example 2-38. The definition of the custom task under the buildSrc directory

```
import org.gradle.api.DefaultTask
import org.gradle.api.tasks.TaskAction

class MySqlTask extends DefaultTask {
  def hostname = 'localhost'
  def port = 3306
  def sql
  def database
  def username = 'root'
  def password = 'password'

  @TaskAction
  def runQuery() {
    def cmd
    if(database) {
      cmd = "mysql -u ${username} -p${password} -h ${hostname}
            -P ${port} ${database} -e "
    }
    else {
```

```
      cmd = "mysql -u ${username} -p${password} -h ${hostname} -P ${port} -e "
    }
    project.exec {
      commandLine = cmd.split().toList() + sql
    }
  }
}
```

Note that the task definition in the `buildSrc` directory is very similar to the code included in the build script in the previous example. However, we now have a robust platform for elaborating on that simple task behavior, growing an object model, writing tests, and doing everything else we normally do when developing software.

 You have four options for where to put your custom Gradle build code. The first is in the build script itself, in a task action block. The second is the `buildSrc` directory as we've shown here. The third is in a separate build script file imported into the main build script. The fourth is in a custom plug-in written in Java or Groovy. Programming Gradle with custom plug-ins will be the topic of a separate volume.

Example 2-39. The structure of a Gradle project with custom code in the buildSrc directory.

```
.
├── build.gradle
├── buildSrc
│   └── src
│       └── main
│           └── groovy
│               └── org
│                   └── gradle
│                       └── example
│                           └── task
│                               └── MySqlTask.groovy
```

Where Do Tasks Come From?

So far, we've been creating tasks by coding them directly, either inside Gradle build scripts or in the `buildSrc` directory as Groovy code. This is a great way to learn about tasks, because it's easy to see all of the moving parts in great detail. However, many of the tasks you use won't be tasks you write; they'll come from plug-ins.

You've already seen an example of this in the section on building Java code. By applying the Java plug-in, the build script automatically inherits a set of tasks whose code you never directly see. You can modify the behavior of these tasks using the task configuration, `doFirst()`, and `doLast()` methods we've covered in this chapter, but you don't have to code them youself. The fact that Gradle is providing you with rich, extensible task functionality whose code you never have to look at—code you invoke through the

Gradle DSL, not through lots of literal Groovy code—is core to Gradle's strategy of provding high extensibility with low complexity.

Gradle also has a few built-in tasks, like `tasks` and `properties`. These aren't provided by any plug-in or any imperative code you write, but are just a standard part of the Gradle DSL. They are covered in the section on the Gradle command line.

Conclusion

We've had a pretty thorough look at tasks in this chapter. We've looked at how to configure them and how to script them, and gotten an idea of how Gradle divides up the work of configuration and execution between two lifecycle phases. We've seen that tasks are first-class Groovy objects with a rich API of their own. We've explored that API just enough to show you how to think about tasks as programmable entities. We also looked at some standard class types that provide real functionality out of the box.

Finally we looked at how to write tasks of your own. Gradle's built-in tasks and plug-ins are enough for many users to script their builds without any custom code, but not always. One of Gradle's fundamental sensibilities is that it should be easy for you to extend your build without cluttering your build scripts with a lot of unmaintainable Groovy code. The custom task examples we looked at illustrated this.

Tasks are the basic unit of build activity in Gradle. There is more to their story than an introduction can cover, but with this chapter under your belt, you're well prepared to start using them and to continue learning about them.

CHAPTER 3

Ant and Gradle

When considering leveraging an existing investment in Apache Ant (*http://ant.apache .org/manual/index.html*), or perhaps using the broad set of tasks that the Ant community has created, Gradle has a great story to tell. Gradle offers a complete superset of Ant. In fact, it makes Gradle's use of Ant simpler than directly using Ant, partly by leveraging Groovy's `AntBuilder` functionality. Gradle brings in everything from the Ant namespace into the Gradle namespace such that using a core Ant task is as easy as calling `ant.<taskname>`.

Discussing the usage of Ant from Gradle provides a great bridge in terms of progressive migration to a pure Gradle strategy. Over time though, we believe you'll desire to standardize on the more powerful Gradle feature set by using native Gradle components or by wraping any Ant behavior in a Gradle plug-in. The latter maintains the value of the functioning Ant behavior while fully enabling build-by-convention throughout the updated Gradle build ecosystem. With full awareness of the quantity of existing Ant infrastructure and value of leveraging it via the new build tool, Gradle ships with a full copy of Ant, thus making Ant's default tasks available to every Gradle build. To aid with this mind-set remapping, we'll discuss how Gradle compares to Ant, providing parallels in the approaches to writing builds and to each tool's unique terminology.

The Vocabulary

Gradle is occasionally described as a Groovy-based Ant. That would be the role that Gant (*http://gant.codehaus.org/*) fills, but Gradle has much more ambitious aims. Gradle offers the flexibility of Ant, which many teams still cherish, but with the dependency management style of Ivy, the intelligent defaults of Maven, the speed and hashing of Git, and the meta-programming power of Groovy. That potent best-of-breed blend is an intrinsic motivator for joining the Gradle movement.

Gradle, like Ant, has a Directed Acyclic Graph (DAG) of tasks in its execution plan. However, Gradle takes better advantage of this graph, and will, in the future, run tasks in parallel that are on discrete paths on the DAG. Gradle also plans to leverage the value of holding this build DAG in memory to run certain graph paths of tasks in parallel across a distributed set of build machines. A prototype visualization tool has even been produced that writes the DAG into a DOT (*http://en.wikipedia.org/wiki/DOT_lan guage*) format, as shown in Figure 3-1.

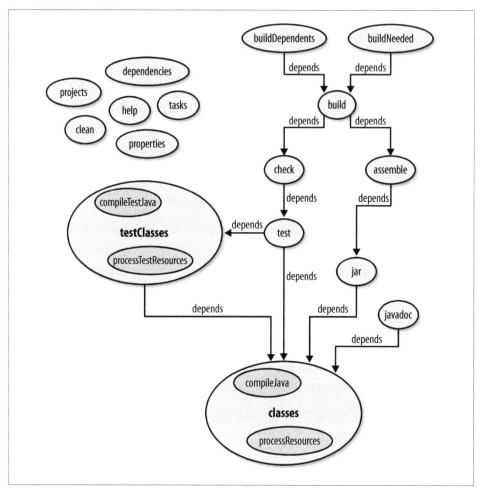

Figure 3-1. DAG of Gradle Tasks

 Both Ant and Gradle use the word task, but with different meanings in each namespace.

Ant uses the word task to indicate one of its executable components (close to what many would call a plug-in in other systems), such as echo. An Ant task can be executed within the context of a target. Gradle defines task to refer to any step of the directed acyclic graph. task in Gradle most closely compares to a target in Ant, but shares some of the benefits of a task in Ant in that a Gradle plug-in can bring several automatic Gradle tasks into the sequence of build steps.

A property in Ant can be compared to a variable in Gradle. In the more powerful Groovy language that Gradle provides, variables can be typeless (as in Ant) or typed, if desired. Variables are available for reference in the parent Gradle project or any subprojects.

Example 3-1. Ant build script defining a property

```
<project>
    <property name="buildoutput" location="output"/>
    <property name="appversion" value="2.1"/>
</project>
```

Example 3-2. Gradle build script defining variables

```
def helloName = "Fird Birfle"
int personAge = 43

task hello << {
    println "Hello ${helloName}. I believe you are ${personAge} years of age."
}
```

Hello Ant

Example 3-3. Ant calling the Ant Echo plug-in with an attribute

```
<project>
    <target name="helloViaAttribute">
        <echo message="hello from Ant"/>
    </target>
</project>
```

Example 3-4. Gradle calling the Ant Echo plug-in with an attribute

```
task hello << {
    String greeting = "hello from Ant"
    ant.echo(message: greeting)
}
```

In Example 3-4, we took a simple string and supplied it to the message parameter of the echo Ant task. It is useful to reiterate that no import-like plug-in statement was needed to make ant (a Groovy AntBuilder instance) available for invocation. Further, no command was needed to make the echo task available for calls. To fully discover which defined fields can be supplied with values, simply refer to the actual Ant Echo task documentation (*http://ant.apache.org/manual/Tasks/echo.html*) since Gradle provides a lightweight wrapper over the Ant implementation.

Making just a minor change to this build, we will additionally use the Echo task's documented ability to accept a message as the sole input as ant.echo(message:

greeting). In Ant's XML form (Example 3-5), this means that the greeting is put between the <echo> task tags, not in a message attribute of the <echo message=""> tag. In Gradle (Example 3-6), the equivalent syntax is passing the greeting string directly into the echo() call without naming the field to which the value should be assigned.

Example 3-5. Ant calling the Ant Echo plug-in with a tag

```
<project>
    <target name="helloViaTag">
        <echo>hello from Ant</echo>
    </target>
</project>
```

Example 3-6. Gradle calling the Ant Echo plug-in with a parameter

```
task hello << {
    String greeting = "hello from Ant"
    ant.echo(greeting)
}
```

This encompasses the basics of using Ant with Gradle, but hardly is the full breadth of such interoperation. Let's go a step further with the importing of custom Ant Tasks, configuration of complex nested Ant structures, and weaving of dependence between Gradle tasks and Ant targets.

Importing Custom Ant Tasks

Using the core Ant tasks from Gradle was easy, but using a custom Ant task is nearly as simple. Just use the taskdef method (*http://ant.apache.org/manual/Tasks/taskdef .html*) on the AntBuilder instance according to the same recipes (*http://ant.apache.org/ manual/Tasks/typedef.html*) that would be used for its Ant invocations.

For the first example, the Checkstyle (*http://checkstyle.sourceforge.net/anttask.html*) Ant task will be loaded from a combination of a properties file and a set of local directory JARs.

Example 3-7. Gradle loading the Checkstyle Ant task via a resource

```
task checkTheStyle << {
    //Load the custom task
    ant.taskdef(resource: 'checkstyletask.properties') {
        classpath {
            fileset(dir: 'libs/checkstyle', includes: '*.jar')
        }
    }

    //Use the custom task
    ant.checkstyle(config: 'src/tools/sun_checks.xml') {
        fileset(dir: 'src')
    }
}
```

In Example 3-7, the entire loading and execution of the custom Ant task happens within a single Gradle task. Using standard Ant capabilities, we fetch the parameters needed to load the Ant task from a properties file named checkstyletask.properties that is contained within one of the jars in the libs/checkstyle directory. It happens to be contained in *checkstyle-5.3-all.jar* and the properties file's contents are minimal, as shown in Example 3-8. There is simply a mapping from the desired task name check style, to bring into the Ant namespace and the fully qualfied class that implements it, com.puppycrawl.tools.checkstyle.CheckStyleTask.

Example 3-8. The checkstyletask.properties file from the Checkstyle JAR

```
checkstyle=com.puppycrawl.tools.checkstyle.CheckStyleTask
```

Lastly, in Example 3-7, we invoke the checkstyle Ant task via a traditional-style method call to ant.checkstyle(...). The nested configurations via config and fileset directly correspond to the Checkstyle Ant equivalents (*http://checkstyle.sourceforge.net/anttask .html*) as if this was being configured with Ant's XML syntax.

As a contrasting example, a custom Ant Task can be loaded using a combination of a Gradle configuration, a declared dependency, and Maven Central repository connectivity.

Example 3-9. Gradle loading the PMD Ant task via a Maven repository and Gradle configuration

```
configurations {
    myPmd
}

dependencies {
    myPmd group: 'pmd', name: 'pmd', version: '4.2.5'
}

repositories {
    mavenCentral()
}

task checkThePMD << {
    ant.taskdef(name: 'myPmdTask', classname: 'net.sourceforge.pmd.ant.PMDTask',
        classpath: configurations.myPmd.asPath)
    ant.myPmdTask(shortFilenames: 'true', failonruleviolation: 'true',
      rulesetfiles: file('src/tools/pmd-basic-rules.xml').toURI().toString()) {
        formatter(type: 'text', toConsole: 'true')
        fileset(dir: 'src/main/java')
    }
}
```

In this more complex example of Example 3-9, we first establish a configuration for myPmd which is a preprocessing step prior to task executions. Configurations were first introduced as a concept in "Task Configuration" on page 15. The configurations closure declares a grouping named myPmd for our subsequent declaration of JAR requirements via the dependencies closure. In the dependencies closure, we once address the `myPmd` grouping and indicate that it should download the PMD JAR as needed. The source of the download is declared as the special repository `mavenCentral()` via the `repositories` closure. Next, the Gradle task `checkThePMD` is established. During the loading of the Ant task definition via `ant.taskdef(///)` call, the JAR downloaded as part of the `myPmd` configuration is added the `myPmdTask` classpath. Last, the `myPmdTask` is invoked via `ant.myPmdTask(...)` with the parameters passed to the Ant task in the same nested manner as Example 3-7.

Complex Ant Configuration

In more complex Ant configurations, there typically are several nested elements in the *build.xml* syntax. Though Gradle provides a native class of tasks for archiving, and specifically a task type of `Zip`, a meaningful and straightforward example of using Ant's zip task can display the native Ant XML configuration and the same independent configuration of said Ant task from within Gradle using the clearer `AntBuilder` notation.

Example 3-10. Ant build.xml zipping the source files

```
<project>
  <target name="zipsourceInAnt">
    <zip destfile='samples-from-ant.zip'>
      <fileset dir= 'samples'>
        <include name='**.txt'/>
      </fileset>
    </zip>
  </target>
</project>
```

In Example 3-10, a very common configuration for preparing a compressed archive using Ant's zip task and XML configuration is shown. It includes all files in any subdirectory of **samples** that ends with the extension *.txt* and writes it into a file named *samples-from-gradle.zip*.

Example 3-11. Gradle using Ant to zip the source files

```
task zipsourceInGradle << {
    ant.zip(destfile: 'samples-from-gradle.zip') {
        fileset(dir: 'samples') {
            include(name: '**.txt')
        }
    }
}
```

In Example 3-11, the more readable Groovy closure notation is used within Gradle to access this same Ant task, offering a one-to-one comparison with the pure Ant execution of the same behavior in Example 3-10.

Importing an Entire Ant Build File

Up to this point, we've dealt with interoperability of Ant and Gradle on a fine-grained level, either calling existing Ant tasks, creating new Ant tasks on the fly, or manipulating the results of Ant task calls with Groovy. But what if you want to bring everything in from an existing Ant build? Gradle handles that without even breaking a sweat.

First, we begin with our traditional Ant project in Example 3-3. Then, inside the Gradle build, we import the Ant targets into a Gradle task.

Example 3-12. Import an entire ant project

```
ant.importBuild 'build.xml'
```

The result is an ability to treat the Ant build's contents as a Gradle task from anywhere else in the Gradle ecosystem. This is an implementation of the Facade pattern; all the utility of the Ant build is maintained, but all the value that Gradle brings to builds is additionally available to the buildmaster.

If we query Gradle for what Gradle tasks it knows about in Example 3-12, the answer will include the helloViaAttribute Ant target.

Example 3-13. Task list from the imported Ant project

```
$ gradle tasks
:tasks

Help tasks
_____
dependencies - Displays the dependencies of root project 'ant-import-to-gradle'.
help - Displays a help message
projects - Displays the subprojects of root project 'ant-import-to-gradle'.
properties - Displays the properties of root project 'ant-import-to-gradle'.
tasks - Displays the tasks in root project 'ant-import-to-gradle'.

Other tasks
_____
helloViaAttribute

To see all tasks and more detail, run with --all.
```

If we run the Gradle project requesting that the helloViaAttribute Gradle task be executed, we'll get the bridged Ant behavior through a pure Gradle interface.

Example 3-14. Sample run of the imported Ant project

```
$ gradle helloViaAttribute
:helloViaAttribute
[ant:echo] hello from Ant
```

Ant Target and Gradle Task Codependence

Ant targets can even participate as a `dependsOn` of Gradle builds, as shown in Example 3-16. Likewise, Ant targets can point to Gradle tasks as `depends` fields, as shown in Example 3-15. The only requirement of the Ant and Gradle integration is that the more capable tool, Gradle, be the point of execution (see Example 3-17). Gradle must drive the initiation of the build, say from from the command line, IDE, or GUI, but can be either the subordinate or dominate player in the actual XML and Gradle build script flow.

Example 3-15. Define an Ant target and have it depend on a Gradle task

```
<project>
  <target name="antStandAloneHello">
    <echo message="A standalone hello from an Ant target"/>
  </target>

  <target name="antHello" depends="beforeTheAntTask">
    <echo message="A dependent hello from the Ant target"/>
  </target>
</project>
```

Example 3-16. Define a task in Gradle that precedes the Ant target

```
ant.importBuild 'build.xml'

defaultTasks = ['antStandAloneHello', 'afterTheAntTask']

task beforeTheAntTask << {
    println "A Gradle task that precedes the Ant target"
}

task afterTheAntTask(dependsOn: "antHello") << {
    println "A Gradle task that precedes the Ant target"
}
```

Example 3-17. Driving the build from Gradle

```
$ gradle

:antStandAloneHello
[ant:echo] A standalone hello from an Ant target

:beforeTheAntTask
A Gradle task that precedes the Ant target

:antHello
[ant:echo] A dependent hello from the Ant target

:afterTheAntTask
A Gradle task that precedes the Ant target

BUILD SUCCESSFUL
```

Using AntBuilder

The power of using Ant with Gradle isn't limited to just the prescribed approaches given thus far. Since the ant object is a full Groovy AntBuilder (*http://groovy.codehaus.org/Using+Ant+from+Groovy*) instance, existing paradigms and constructs from the Groovy language (*http://groovy.codehaus.org/*) can be used here. Though comprehensive knowledge of Groovy is not a prerequisite, any increased understanding of Groovy has a direct benefit to the authoring of Gradle build files since Gradle supports the gamut of Groovy syntax.

For example, to list the contents of a directory using an Ant FileScanner and Ant FileSet, just use the ant instance with Groovy closure nesting for Ant subelement access, as shown in Example 3-18.

Example 3-18. Scan folders with Ant and iterate over the results in Gradle

```
task echoDirListViaAntBuilder() {
    description = 'Uses the built-in AntBuilder instance to echo and list files'
    //Docs: http://ant.apache.org/manual/Types/fileset.html

    //Echo the Gradle project name via the ant echo plugin
    ant.echo(message: project.name)
    ant.echo(path)
    ant.echo("${projectDir}/samples")

    //Gather list of files in a subdirectory
    ant.fileScanner{
        fileset(dir:"samples")
    }.each{
        //Print each file to screen with the CWD (projectDir) path removed.
        println it.toString() - "${projectDir}"
    }
}
```

The power of Groovy's operators can also be leveraged inside AntBuilder calls, such as using the regular expression matcher inside an evaluation of all System properties in Example 3-19. The spread *, elvis ?:, and other Groovy operators (*http://groovy.code haus.org/Operators*) can all be applied directly or to subcomponents of the ant instance for a high code-to-effect ratio. With almost no ceremony, the ==~ "firecracker" operator is used in Example 3-19 to query for regular expression matches of a string, charsToFind.

Example 3-19. Use the Groovy regular expression operator in an AntBuilder output

```
task echoSystemPropertiesWithRegEx() {
    description = "Uses Groovy's regex matching to find a match in System properties"

    def charsToFind = 'sun'

    println "SYSTEM PROPERTIES"
    System.properties.each{
        ant.echo("Does '${it}' contain '${charsToFind}': " +
        (it ==~ ".*${charsToFind}.*"))
```

```
    }
}
```

In the ultimate combination, a progressive migration from Ant to Gradle can be greatly
aided by the ability to bring Ant classpaths into the Gradle space. Example 3-20 dem-
onstrates the establishment of two paths in the Ant realm, and then the consumption
of those paths in the Gradle space, including using them as repositories in Example 3-21.

Example 3-20. Ant defining two paths

```
<project>
    <!-- Classpath created by Ant, then used by Gradle -->
    <path id="antPathToLibs1" location="antlibs"/>
    <path id="antPathToLibs2" location="antlibs"/>
</project>
```

On the *build.gradle* side of this example, the use of the * "spread" operator demon-
strates how to `println repositories*.name` all the repositories name fields in a single
statement instead of three.

Example 3-21. Use the Ant path references inside the Gradle build

```
ant.importBuild 'build.xml'

defaultTasks = ['gradleBuild']

////////////////////////////////////////////////////////////////////
// Gradle paths retrieved from Ant and then built using a Gradle task
repositories {
    flatDir name: 'localRepository1', dirs: ant.references['antPathToLibs1']
    flatDir name: 'localRepository2', dirs: ant.references.antPathToLibs2
    flatDir name: 'localRepository3', dirs: "antlibs"
}

task gradleBuild << {
    //Set classpath to include the JAR
    println "The repositories bridged from Ant to Gradle are:"
    println repositories*.name

    println repositories.localRepository1

    println repositories['localRepository2']

    println "localRepository3 class = " + repositories.localRepository3.class
    println "localRepository3 name = " + repositories.localRepository3.name
    println "localRepository3 latest = " + repositories.localRepository3.latest
    println "localRepository3 ivyPatterns = " + repositories.localRepository3.ivyPatterns
    println "localRepository3 artifactPatterns =
        " + repositories.localRepository3.artifactPatterns
    println "localRepository3 checkconsistency =
        " + repositories.localRepository3.checkconsistency
    println "localRepository3 m2compatible =
        " + repositories.localRepository3.m2compatible
```

```
    println "localRepository3 methods =
        " + repositories.localRepository3.metaClass.methods*.name.sort().unique()
}
```

The converse use case is also possible and easy. Paths can be established in Gradle, as shown in Example 3-23, and then consumed in an Ant target in Example 3-22 that even depends on the antPathsInjectedByGradle Gradle task.

Example 3-22. Ant build file that consumes the Gradle paths

```
<project>
    <!-- Classpath created by Gradle, then used by Ant -->
    <path refid="gradlePathToLibs1"/>
    <path refid="gradlePathToLibs2"/>
    <path refid="gradlePathToLibs3"/>

    <!-- Echo one of the gradle paths injected into the Ant build -->
    <target name="antBuild" depends="antPathsInjectedByGradle">
      <property name="gradlePathToLibs1AsProperty" refid="gradlePathToLibs1"/>
      <echo message="gradlePathToLibs1 = ${gradlePathToLibs1AsProperty}"/>

      <property name="gradlePathToLibs2AsProperty" refid="gradlePathToLibs2"/>
      <echo message="gradlePathToLibs2 = ${gradlePathToLibs2AsProperty}"/>

      <property name="gradlePathToLibs3AsProperty" refid="gradlePathToLibs3"/>
      <echo message="gradlePathToLibs3 = ${gradlePathToLibs3AsProperty}"/>

    </target>
</project>
```

Example 3-23. The Gradle build file that injects the build paths into Ant

```
ant.importBuild 'build.xml'

defaultTasks = ['antBuild']

//////////////////////////////////////////////////////////////////////////
// Ant paths injected by Gradle and then built using an Ant goal
task antPathsInjectedByGradle << {
    ant.path(id: 'gradlePathToLibs1', location: 'gradlelibs')
    // or
    ant.references.gradlePathToLibs2 = ant.path(location: 'gradlelibs')
    // or
    ant.references['gradlePathToLibs3'] =
        ant.path(location: file('gradlelibs').absolutePath)

    println "This task injects Gradle paths into the AntBuilder"
}

antBuild.doLast {
    // No antBuild Task needs to be explicitly constructed
    // antBuild task is created by the build.xml import
    println "This Ant goal was converted to a Gradle task by the ant.importBuild call"
}
```

A Harmonic Duo

Over the course of this chapter, the examples have demonstrated the simplicity of integrating Ant with Gradle. The purpose of the cross-tool calls can either be that of a careful stepwise migration to Gradle, or the filling in for an absent Gradle plug-in with a well-established Ant equivalent. Gradle's build tool compatibility represents an understanding of the real world of software engineering: migrations don't always happen overnight and bridges to legacy technologies make Gradle an option for many more teams and projects.

CHAPTER 4

Maven and Gradle

Up to this point, you've seen the very light footprint of Gradle. You might be convinced it is the way to go for new projects. However, only a very few of us are blessed with the wide-open choices afforded to a greenfield project. The majority of us have an existing build system in place and the mandate to maintain continuity of the build. We might even have downstream clients of our JAR, WAR, and EAR binary artifacts. Gradle would only be a logical successor to Maven if it offered a very thoughtful path to both migration and integration from the world's largest open source build system. It certainly does. Let's take a look.

Cue Graven?

First, let's provide a bearing on the attitude of Gradle. It is not the next incremental step after Maven. It is not just another Domain Specific Language (DSL) on top of the existing build tooling with which we are already familiar. It is, in fact, a progression of selected ideas of our existing build tools. Gradle brings only the best ideas forward and leaves behind the ones that fell short of their intended mark. That is a generic set of claims. Let's proceed to specifics.

 It would be easy to think of Polyglot Maven (*http://polyglot.sonatype .org*) as an equivalent to Gradle, but alas, the constraints that apply to Maven apply to Polyglot Maven as well, just sans the angle brackets of XML. Gradle aims to be something more powerful than its predecessor tools in the build space.

Gradle takes the *convention over configuration* and *consistently named artifact* concepts and brings them forward from the playbook of Maven. Gradle also implements a *strong domain model* that is easily programmatically accessible. Though often cited, it is debatable as to whether Maven actually has a strong model or merely a strong authoring language in the form of an XSD-compliant XML file.

Diving to a deeper level of precision, Gradle takes the coordinates, including `groupId`, `artifactId`, and `version`, in producing new build artifacts. It also offers a bridge, in the form of a dependency management definition graph, to Maven and Ivy artifact repositories without demanding remote repositories. This provides connectivity to open-source hosted binaries on sites like *Maven Central*, Java.net, and *Clojars*, just to name a few. But the flexibility of Gradle also allows for the very valid use case in which dependency binaries are stored alongside the source in version control, whether for legal or technical reasons. In the example of the ultimate flexibility allowed in Gradle, a default mapping is provided to the community-known dependency (classpath) scopes of Maven, but Gradle users can establish custom dependency scopes should the need arise.

That is a solid overview of what has been brought forward from the forge of the past decade of build tool experiments and field testing. But what was intentionally omitted? Gradle leaves behind the expensive XML format. It is pure Groovy goodness. We'll also leave behind the strict, predefined lifecycle of Maven and the absence of a lifecycle with Ant. Both are too far toward the ends of the spectrum of control and chaos, respectively. Gradle will instead replace the strict Maven lifecycle with task defaults set via common plug-ins such as `java`. Even with convenient defaults, Gradle offers a painless and lightweight way to extend the plug-in-supplied task sequence with additional steps that fit your build's unique needs.

The Maven POM and Gradle Build

With the big picture established, let's take a piecewise approach to comparing Maven and Gradle. We will start with a reminder of the appearance of a barest bones Maven POM.

Example 4-1. The smallest possible Maven pom.xml

```xml
<!-- The smallest possible Maven POM.xml -->
<project>
  <modelVersion>4.0.0</modelVersion>
  <groupId>com.gradleware.samples</groupId>
  <artifactId>sample01-barestbones</artifactId>
  <version>0.0.1-SNAPSHOT</version>
</project>
```

While often desirable to have the formal vectors of `groupId`, `artifactId`, and `version` for a build, there are equally times where it is overkill. No allowance is made for that in Maven. You must provide all the fields. Adding a final bit of cruft, you also need the `modelVersion` field, just in case Maven should ever decide to expand its vocabulary of tags (though it hasn't since the release of Maven 2.0 in 2004).

Earlier in the book, we showed you just how simple it was to get started with Gradle, so we will leave the simplicity of that first Gradle build file to the earlier example, "The Hello World Build File" on page 6. We will use, as our first comparison with Maven, a Gradle build file in Example 4-2 that defines a few attributes and can produce a JAR, a common final product of a Java build.

Example 4-2. The simplest Maven equivalent build.gradle file

```
apply plugin: 'java'
```

That one line Gradle build file in Example 4-2, when executed with a mere `gradle build` from the command line, performed the following actions:

- Downloaded any declared dependencies (none) to *~/.gradle/cache*
- Compiled the code in *src/main/java*
- Wrote the class files into *build/classes/main*
- Attempted to compile and run any unit tests (none)
- Wrote unit test results in XML format to *build/test-results/*
- Wrote an HTML-formatted unit test report to *build/reports/tests/*
- Generated a *MANIFEST.MF* in *build/tmp/jar/MANIFEST.MF*
- Compressed the `.class` files along with the *MANIFEST.MF* into a JAR in *build/libs/maven-gradle-comparison-simple.jar*

The described actions taken by Gradle are made evident by examining the files in the structure of the `output` directory.

Example 4-3. Listing of the build subdirectory from the Example 4-2 Gradle build project

```
build
├── classes
│   └── main
│       └── Main.class
├── dependency-cache
├── libs
│   └── maven-gradle-comparison-simple.jar
├── reports
│   └── tests
│       ├── css3-pie-1.0beta3.htc
│       ├── index.html
│       ├── report.js
│       └── style.css
├── test-results
└── tmp
    └── jar
        └── MANIFEST.MF
```

Maven Goals, Gradle Tasks

The aforementioned minimalistic Gradle build also offered many of the tasks (nee Maven goals) we would have at our disposal with Maven. Let's examine the names of these tasks by asking Gradle what it can offer us by invoking the **tasks** task.

Example 4-4. Querying Gradle for the available tasks

```
$ gradle tasks

Build tasks
-----------
assemble - Assembles all Jar, War, Zip, and Tar archives.
build - Assembles and tests this project.
buildDependents - Assembles and tests this project and
  all projects that depend on it.
buildNeeded - Assembles and tests this project and
  all projects it depends on.
classes - Assembles the main classes.
clean - Deletes the build directory.
jar - Assembles a jar archive containing the main classes.
testClasses - Assembles the test classes.

Documentation tasks
-------------------
javadoc - Generates Javadoc API documentation
  for the main source code.

Help tasks
----------
dependencies - Displays the dependencies of
  root project 'maven-gradle-comparison-simple'.
help - Displays a help message
projects - Displays the subprojects of
  root project 'maven-gradle-comparison-simple'.
properties - Displays the properties of
  root project 'maven-gradle-comparison-simple'.
tasks - Displays the tasks in
  root project 'maven-gradle-comparison-simple'.

Verification tasks
------------------
check - Runs all checks.
test - Runs the unit tests.
```

We see that tasks to clean, build, test, and JAR the project's code are included via the simple inclusion of the **java** plug-in.

The Standard Maven Coordinates, Gradle Properties

That comparison of a one line `build.gradle` to the most minimal `pom.xml` was valid, but not completely controlled in the metadata values for `groupId`, `artifactId`, and `version`. In Gradle, the `groupId` is known just as `group`, the `artifactId` is known as `name`, and the `version` is identically `version`. Formally, each of these kind of fields is known as a *property* in Gradle since we are saving state in POJO objects under the hood.

Table 4-1. Maven-to-Gradle Coordinate Mappings and Defaults

Maven Coordinate	Gradle Property	Gradle Default
groupId	group	blank
artifactId	name or archivesBaseName	project's directory name
version	version	unspecified
name	N/A	N/A
description	description	null

Growing our Gradle example to a more robust Maven POM equivalent, we'll add the *version* field. This is common in Gradle builds, even in the absence of the other *group* and *artifact* coordinates. The *version* property is defined in the Gradle DSL reference (*http://www.gradle.org/latest/docs/dsl/org.gradle.api.Project.html*) and is present in every type of build, even without the *java* plug-in. The `archivesBaseName` value is appended to the end of the produced JAR.

Example 4-5. Gradle build that includes a version number for the output artifact

```
apply plugin: 'java'
version = '0.0.1-SNAPSHOT'
```

When we run this refined build, take note that the output JAR in the libs directory is now named `maven-gradle-comparison-withattrs-0.0.1-SNAPSHOT.jar`, whereas it was previously named the less precise, `maven-gradle-comparison-simple.jar` in Example 4-2. Recall that the artifact name defaults to the project's directory name if no more precisely desired value is supplied as shown in Table 4-1.

Example 4-6. Directory listing of output from the version-specified Gradle build

```
$ tree
```

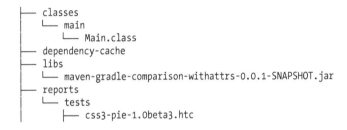

```
├── classes
│   └── main
│       └── Main.class
├── dependency-cache
├── libs
│   └── maven-gradle-comparison-withattrs-0.0.1-SNAPSHOT.jar
├── reports
│   └── tests
│       ├── css3-pie-1.0beta3.htc
```

```
│        ├── index.html
│        ├── report.js
│        └── style.css
├── test-results
└── tmp
    └── jar
        └── MANIFEST.MF
```

Next, using the knowledge gained in Table 4-1, we can control all values of the coordinates that would typically be set in a Maven-participating project. Note that the name field presented by the very foundation of Gradle is only mutable in the *settings.gradle* file (*http://www.gradle.org/latest/docs/dsl/org.gradle.api.Project.html*), and if not supplied in *settings.gradle*, the `archivesBaseName` property is assigned a value instead. The *archivesBaseName* property is brought into existence by the `java` plug-in.

 Gradle 1.0 aims to simplify the field name mapping, doing away with archivesBaseName, and possibly providing a top level closure to configure the project's Maven-equivalent coordinates.

Up to this point, we've only used the `java` plug-in. Though many of these features look Maven-like in their naming and function, these are behaviors desired by nearly any Java project, even standalone single-JAR Java applications. The consistent location of Gradle's source directories (*src/main/java*) and the specification of the artifact's `group`, `name`, and `version` metadata is useful, even without the aim of uploading an artifact to a remote repository.

The most visible Gradle win thus far is having the properties at the top level of the build file with slightly simplified property names rather than the XML nesting of Maven. Keep reading. The wins are about to get more significant.

More Gradle Properties

Having introduced one plug-in thus far, you might be wondering what range of properties are available to control. Gradle offers an easy always-available task named `properties` to list the fields and values of the current build. Let's echo all the Gradle properties to the console with the `-r` or `--properties` flag.

Example 4-7. Gradle Properties of a "hello world" build

```
$ gradle properties

additionalProperties: {}
all: [task ':helloWorld']
allprojects: [root project 'minimal-build-file']
ant: org.gradle.api.internal.project.DefaultAntBuilder@5057f57f
antBuilderFactory: org.gradle.api.internal.project.DefaultAntBuilderFactory@114562c5
artifacts: org.gradle.api.internal.artifacts.dsl.DefaultArtifactHandler@23bf8cd5
```

```
asDynamicObject: org.gradle.api.internal.DynamicObjectHelper@30c26c8f
asMap: {helloWorld=task ':helloWorld'}
buildDir: /minimal-build-file/build
buildDirName: build
buildFile: /minimal-build-file/build.gradle
buildScriptSource: org.gradle.groovy.scripts.UriScriptSource@111edceb
buildscript: org.gradle.api.internal.initialization.DefaultScriptHandler@7fb2380e
childProjects: {}
class: class org.gradle.api.internal.project.DefaultProject_Decorated
classGenerator: org.gradle.api.internal.AsmBackedClassGenerator@709a1411
configurations: org.gradle.api.internal.artifacts.configurations.
  DefaultConfigurationContainer_Decorated@69d4eeb5
convention: org.gradle.api.internal.plugins.DefaultConvention@71cbd4f7
conventionMapping: org.gradle.api.internal.ConventionAwareHelper@1aa632be
defaultTasks: []
dependencies: org.gradle.api.internal.artifacts.dsl.dependencies.
  DefaultDependencyHandler@d44752d
dependsOnProjects: []
depth: 0
description: null
displayName: task container
fileResolver: org.gradle.api.internal.file.BaseDirConverter@56d99277
gradle: build 'minimal-build-file'
group:
helloWorld: task ':helloWorld'
implicitTasks: org.gradle.api.internal.tasks.DefaultTaskContainer_Decorated@384ab40a
inheritedScope: org.gradle.api.internal.
  DynamicObjectHelper$InheritedDynamicObject@388a2006
logger: org.gradle.api.logging.Logging$LoggerImpl@521c5cd7
logging: org.gradle.logging.internal.DefaultLoggingManager@3821b42f
metaClass: org.codehaus.groovy.runtime.HandleMetaClass@5b76de14[
  groovy.lang.MetaClassImpl@5b76de14[
    class org.gradle.api.internal.project.DefaultProject_Decorated]]
module: org.gradle.api.internal.artifacts.DefaultModule@59a51312
name: minimal-build-file
parent: null
parentIdentifier: null
path: :
plugins: org.gradle.api.internal.plugins.DefaultProjectsPluginContainer@5608a6fc
project: root project 'minimal-build-file'
projectDir: /minimal-build-file
projectEvaluationBroadcaster: ProjectEvaluationListener broadcast
projectEvaluator: org.gradle.configuration.DefaultProjectEvaluator@6212f195
projectRegistry: org.gradle.api.internal.project.DefaultProjectRegistry@5e1558dc
properties: {...}
repositories: org.gradle.api.internal.artifacts.dsl.
  DefaultRepositoryHandler_Decorated@ba3bc8c
repositoryHandlerFactory: org.gradle.api.internal.artifacts.dsl.
  SharedConventionRepositoryHandlerFactory@41ed54a0
rootDir: /minimal-build-file
rootProject: root project 'minimal-build-file'
rules: []
services: ProjectInternalServiceRegistry
standardOutputCapture: org.gradle.logging.internal.DefaultLoggingManager@3821b42f
state: org.gradle.api.internal.project.ProjectStateInternal@594560cf
```

```
status: release
subprojects: []
tasks: org.gradle.api.internal.tasks.DefaultTaskContainer_Decorated@5e20dcb7
type: interface org.gradle.api.Task
typeDisplayName: task
version: unspecified
```

The properties listed here have a wide range of *rare* to *common* in their frequency of being configured. Many have sensible defaults, such as **status** being set to **release**, and are thus only occasionally tuned to an alternative value.

Adding the **java** plug-in as per the original sample build file introduces the *additional* properties shown in Example 4-8.

Example 4-8. Java plug-in introduced properties

```
apiDocTitle: maven-gradle-comparison-simple API
archivesBaseName: maven-gradle-comparison-simple
assemble: task ':assemble'
build: task ':build'
buildDependents: task ':buildDependents'
buildNeeded: task ':buildNeeded'
buildTasks: [build]
check: task ':check'
classes: task ':classes'
clean: task ':clean'
compileJava: task ':compileJava'
compileTestJava: task ':compileTestJava'
dependencyCacheDir: /maven-gradle-comparison-simple/build/dependency-cache
dependencyCacheDirName: dependency-cache
distsDir: /maven-gradle-comparison-simple/build/distributions
distsDirName: distributions
docsDir: /maven-gradle-comparison-simple/build/docs
docsDirName: docs
jar: task ':jar'
javadoc: task ':javadoc'
libsDir: /maven-gradle-comparison-simple/build/libs
libsDirName: libs
manifest: org.gradle.api.java.archives.internal.DefaultManifest@7a66998f
metaInf: []
processResources: task ':processResources'5
processTestResources: task ':processTestResources'
rebuildTasks: [clean, build]
reportsDir: /maven-gradle-comparison-simple/build/reports
reportsDirName: reports
rules: [
  Rule: Pattern: build<ConfigurationName>: Assembles the artifacts
    of a configuration.,
  Rule: Pattern: upload<ConfigurationName>: Assembles and uploads the
    artifacts belonging to a configuration.,
  Rule: Pattern: clean<TaskName>: Cleans the output files of a task.]
runtimeClasspath: file collection
sourceCompatibility: 1.5
sourceSets: org.gradle.api.internal.tasks.DefaultSourceSetContainer_Decorated@2850a492
targetCompatibility: 1.5
```

```
test: task ':test'
testClasses: task ':testClasses'
testReportDir: /maven-gradle-comparison-simple/build/reports/tests
testReportDirName: tests
testResultsDir: /maven-gradle-comparison-simple/build/test-results
testResultsDirName: test-results
```

Dependencies

It is rare to see a project stand alone, independent of any third party or in-house library. It almost goes without saying that a Java project will use some open source components such as *log4j* or *commons-collections*. Gradle offers both an Ivy and Maven dependency and repository compatibility layer, allowing for very simplistic and flexible specification of dependencies and repositories.

A library is declared as a desired *external dependency* by a one-line listing in a closure named dependencies. The most concise form of expressing this is a colon-separated list of fields in a single string.

Example 4-9. Dependency on a library in the most concise syntax

```
dependencies {
    compile 'commons-beanutils:commons-beanutils:1.8.3'
}
```

A more verbose form preferred by some, but accomplishing the same thing, is a field-by-field list.

Example 4-10. Test compilation dependency on the latest 4.8.x version of JUnit

```
dependencies {
    testCompile group: 'junit', name: 'junit', version: '4.8.+'
    compile group: 'commons-beanutils', name: 'commons-beanutils', version: '1.8.3'
}
```

What are these testCompile and compile phrases we see in Example 4-10? They are the scopes for which the declared *external dependencies* are to apply.

With the java plug-in introduced, there are six available scopes (or configurations to use the precise Gradle term) to which dependencies can be assigned. Those six are as follows:

- compile
- default
- testCompile
- testRuntime
- archives
- runtime

However, unlike the fixed scopes of Maven, we have more flexibility with Gradle, to the objective of providing greater build flexibility. New scopes, such as **groovy**, can be introduced by a plug-in. Here we see an additional library being added to the **groovy** scope.

Example 4-11. Displaying dependency assignment to scopes

```
apply plugin: 'java'
apply plugin: 'groovy'

group = 'com.gradleware.samples'
version = '0.0.1-SNAPSHOT'

repositories {
    mavenCentral()
}

dependencies {
    testCompile 'junit:junit:4.8.2'
    compile 'commons-beanutils:commons-beanutils:1.8.3'
    //groovy 'mule:mule-extras-groovy:1.+'
      // ^ The "+" flexible definition of a version
      //   requires Internet access
    groovy 'mule:mule-extras-groovy:1.1.1'
}
```

The output of asking Gradle to list the dependencies shows that indeed, the new library lives beneath the **groovy** scope, but also scopes that logically need what was made available to **groovy**. That includes compile, default, runtime, testCompile, and compile.

Example 4-12. Displaying dependency assignment to scopes

```
$ gradle dependencies

archives - Configuration for the default artifacts.
No dependencies

compile - Classpath for compiling the sources.
+--- mule:mule-extras-groovy:1.1.1 [default]
\--- commons-beanutils:commons-beanutils:1.8.3 [default]
     \--- commons-logging:commons-logging:1.1.1 [compile,master,runtime]

default - Configuration for the default artifacts and their dependencies.
+--- mule:mule-extras-groovy:1.1.1 [default]
\--- commons-beanutils:commons-beanutils:1.8.3 [default]
     \--- commons-logging:commons-logging:1.1.1 [compile,master,runtime]

groovy - The groovy libraries to be used for this Groovy project.
\--- mule:mule-extras-groovy:1.1.1 [default]

runtime - Classpath for running the compiled sources.
+--- mule:mule-extras-groovy:1.1.1 [default]
\--- commons-beanutils:commons-beanutils:1.8.3 [default]
     \--- commons-logging:commons-logging:1.1.1 [compile,master,runtime]
```

```
testCompile - Classpath for compiling the test sources.
+--- mule:mule-extras-groovy:1.1.1 [default]
+--- commons-beanutils:commons-beanutils:1.8.3 [default]
|    \--- commons-logging:commons-logging:1.1.1 [compile,master,runtime]
\--- junit:junit:4.8.2 [default]

testRuntime - Classpath for running the test sources.
+--- mule:mule-extras-groovy:1.1.1 [default]
+--- commons-beanutils:commons-beanutils:1.8.3 [default]
|    \--- commons-logging:commons-logging:1.1.1 [compile,master,runtime]
\--- junit:junit:4.8.2 [default]
```

Gradle offers programmatic access to all elements of the *model* that represents the ultimate build plan. A simple showcase of this access is the printing of the dependencies to screen in Example 4-13. Iterating through all dependencies can take simultaneous advantage of the **dependencies** object and the Groovy **each** method that accepts a closure. The contents of the closure **println**s the result, but could also perform manipulation or testing of the nodes, searching for a given pattern and conditionally acting on its inclusion.

Example 4-13. Print all dependencies

```
task printDeps(dependsOn: build) << {
    configurations*.dependencies.each { println it }
}
```

Repositories

The concept of retrieving libraries, source JARs, dependency metadata, and JavaDoc archives is an expected foundation of any modern build tool. Maven has such capabilities (*http://maven.apache.org/guides/introduction/introduction-to-repositories.html*) at its very core. Ant (*http://ant.apache.org/*), though the older of the JVM build tools, has been supplemented by the Ivy (*http://ant.apache.org/ivy/*) subproject to accomplish exactly this. Ivy offers both a namesake format as well as compatibility with Maven repositories. Gradle provides a bridge implementation to equally consume Ivy- or Maven-formatted repositories.

Gradle goes far beyond just offering an API bridge to Ivy and Maven. It provides a Gradle-flavored DSL for both aforementioned dependency tools that make working with repositories quite simple.

First, a demonstration of adding the mother of all repositories, :16:[Maven Central] in Example 4-14. The ever-important **Maven Central** has its own predefined method **mavenCentral()**.

Example 4-14. Using Maven Central with Gradle

```
repositories {
    mavenCentral()
}
```

Since many organizations will need to additionally, or as a replacement, depend on a company-internal repository, that is equally easy with an addition of a URL to the mavenRepo configuration element of repositories in Example 4-15.

Example 4-15. A custom URL

```
repositories {
    mavenRepo(urls: 'http://repo.gradle.org/gradle/libs-releases-local')
}
```

If your project needs a true Ivy repository (*http://ant.apache.org/ivy/*) with resolution customization, then Gradle is up to the task with a convenient ivy closure syntax, as shown in Example 4-16.

Example 4-16. An Ivy repository

```
repositories {
    ivy {
        name = 'ivyRepo'
        artifactPattern "http://repo.gradleware.org/[organisation]/[module]/
[revision]/[artifact]-[revision].[ext]"
    }
}
```

What if your dependencies aren't yet in a standard repository, but rather are stored in a custom folder (*http://gradle.org/current/docs/userguide/dependency_management .html#sec:repositories*) alongside your project? Gradle handles that with ease via the add() method and a FileSystemResolver(), as shown in Example 4-17.

Example 4-17. A filesystem-based custom repo

```
repositories {
    add(new FileSystemResolver()) {
        name = "repo"
        addArtifactPattern("$rootDir/repo/[organization]/[module]-[revision].[ext]")
        addIvyPattern("$rootDir/repo/[organization]/ivy-[module]-[revision].xml")
        checkmodified = true
    }
}
```

Lastly, what if you haven't even begun your versioning and standardization of the names of your project's artifacts? What if they are just a series of JARs in a single flat subdirectory? It should be no surprise by now that Gradle also has a convenient syntax for this requirement, called flat, as shown in Example 4-18.

Example 4-18. A flat filesystem repo

```
repositories {
    // A single directory added to a custom-named repositories grouping.
    flatDir name: 'localDiskRepo', dirs: 'lib'

    // And a more convenient syntax for multiple directories
    added to the default grouping.
    flatDir dirs: ['graphiclibs', 'guilibs']
}
```

Unit Testing

Unit testing is enabled as soon as the `java` plug-in is included in a Gradle build script. There's no additional effort to enable the `testCompile` dependency scope and `test Classes` task. However, the selection of a particular testing framework library still needs to be stated via the `dependencies` section of the build.gradle file. This facilitates compiled tests being able to reference *JUnit* or *TestNG* annotations or base classes.

Example 4-19. Enabling compilation of unit tests

```
apply plugin: 'java'
apply plugin: 'maven'

group = 'com.gradleware.samples'
version = '0.0.1-SNAPSHOT'

repositories {
    mavenCentral()
}

dependencies {
    testCompile group: 'junit', name: 'junit', version: '4.8.+'
}
```

The unit tests can be compiled via the `testClasses` task.

Example 4-20. Compiling unit tests

```
$ gradle testClasses

:compileJava
:processResources
:classes
:compileTestJava
:processTestResources
:testClasses

BUILD SUCCESSFUL
```

However, it is far more common to both compile and execute the tests in one seamless step. Simply invoke the `test` task to do this.

Example 4-21. Running unit tests

```
$ gradle test

:compileJava
:processResources
:classes
:compileTestJava
:processTestResources
:testClasses
:test

BUILD SUCCESSFUL
```

The raw reports from the execution of the unit tests are written to the *build/test-results* directory and the distilled HTML output is written to the *build/reports/tests* directory.

Example 4-22. Unit test execution output

```
build
├── reports
│   └── tests
│           ├── TestMain.html
│           ├── css3-pie-1.0beta3.htc
│           ├── default-package.html
│           ├── index.html
│           ├── report.js
│           └── style.css
└── test-results
        └── TEST-TestMain.xml
```

A sample HTML report from this unit test is handsomely formatted as shown in Figure 4-1.

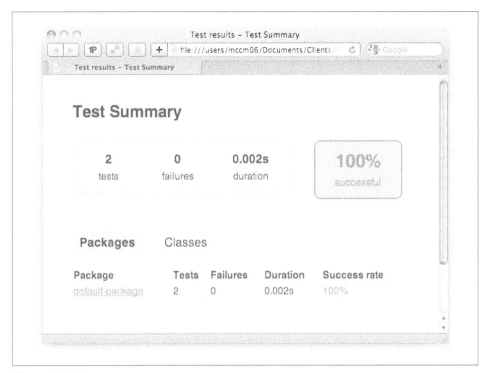

Figure 4-1. Unit test report

Multiple Source Directories

In Maven, it takes hackery and the help of the build-helper-maven-plug-in (*http://mojo .codehaus.org/build-helper-maven-plugin/add-source-mojo.html*) to add more than one source directory. This is one of those cases where constraints are helpful, right up to the point that you need to break them. Then, Maven causes you great pain to circumvent the limitation for your possibly very valid engineering reason. This is ultimately because the internal model of Maven is limited to just one source folder.

On the other hand, Gradle offers you the convention of a single source folder, named *src/main/java*, but lets you add more directories very easily, should your build's design call for it. A `sourceSets` entry named `main` is registered by default with the `java` plug-in and since that is a collection, we can simply modify it to give it an additional directory to scan during compilation, as shown in Example 4-23.

Example 4-23. Code example of multiple source directories

```
apply plugin: 'java'

sourceSets.main.java.srcDirs =
  ["src/main/java", "srcAdditional/main/java"]
```

```
// This add (while maintaining the default src/main/java)
// can also be accomplished with a call:
sourceSets.main.java.srcDirs 'srcAdditionalTwo/main/java'
```

Default Tasks

Default tasks are easy in Gradle. They are more than just a convenience for the build user, but rather a means to communicate which task was intended by the author to be the primary function of this build.

There was no facility for more than one default goal in Maven 1 (*http://jira.codehaus .org/browse/MAVEN-1663*) or Maven 2 (*http://jira.codehaus.org/browse/MNG-1144*); however, this was fixed in Maven 3, closing the associated defect after five long years.

To implement a default goal in Maven, include a single `<defaultGoal>` tag-wrapped task (Maven 1, 2) or space-separated list of tasks (Maven 3).

Example 4-24. Default goals for Maven 3

```
<build>
    <defaultGoal>clean install</defaultGoal>
</build>
```

Gradle has nearly the same facility, but has included support for multiple default tasks from the get-go.

Example 4-25. Default tasks for Gradle

```
apply plugin: 'java'

//Alternate approach 1
//defaultTasks = ['clean', 'build']

//Alternate approach 2
//defaultTasks 'clean'

//Approach 3
defaultTasks 'clean', 'build'
```

The Maven Plug-in

It isn't until the point at which we need to publish a Maven *pom.xml* file for our project to participate in Maven-compatible dependency resolution that we need to involve Gradle's *Maven plug-in*.

The `archivesBaseName` property introduced by the `java` plug-in can be consumed by the newly introduced `maven` plug-in in controlling the value written out as the `artifactId` in the generated *pom.xml* file. If left empty, the project's directory name is used, as per the defaults table.

A Gradle build file need only specify all the Maven coordinates if it wants precise control over each value. The full set of coordinates will be generated into the pom.xml file no matter what, simply with default values if not explicitly set.

Example 4-26. Gradle build that specifies all the usual Maven coordinates

```
apply plugin: 'java'
apply plugin: 'maven'

group = 'com.gradleware.samples'
// archivesBaseName is, via the java plugin, then the Maven plugin,
//   ultimately setting artifactId for the Maven POM generation
// project.name is used by default, but is immutable
archivesBaseName = 'sample01-barestbones'
version = '0.0.1-SNAPSHOT'
description ="A sample project that uses the Maven plug-in and defines many attributes."
```

Example 4-27. Running the pom.xml generation process

```
$ gradle install

:compileJava
:processResources
:classes
:jar
:install

BUILD SUCCESSFUL
```

Example 4-28. Build directory listing from the fully coordinate-specified Gradle build

```
$ tree

build
├── libs
│    └── sample01-barestbones-0.0.1-SNAPSHOT.jar
├── poms
        └── pom-default.xml
```

Example 4-29. The produced pom.xml file

```
<?xml version="1.0" encoding="UTF-8"?>
<project xsi:schemaLocation=
    "http://maven.apache.org/POM/4.0.0 http://maven.apache.org/xsd/maven-4.0.0.xsd"
    xmlns="http://maven.apache.org/POM/4.0.0"
    xmlns:xsi="http://www.w3.org/2001/XMLSchema-instance">
  <modelVersion>4.0.0</modelVersion>
  <groupId>com.gradleware.samples</groupId>
  <artifactId>sample01-barestbones</artifactId>
  <version>0.0.1-SNAPSHOT</version>
</project>
```

Alternatively, a configuration closure can be used to set the same information for the benefit of the generated *pom.xml* file.

Example 4-30. Using Configuration to control the generated POM

```
apply plugin: 'java'
apply plugin: 'maven'

defaultTasks = ['install']

configure(install.repositories.mavenInstaller) {
    pom.project {
        groupId 'com.gradleware.samples'
        artifactId 'sample02-barestbones'
        version '0.0.1-SNAPSHOT'
        description ='A sample project that uses the Maven plug-in
                    and defines many attributes.'
    }
}
```

In either the approach of setting Gradle properties or authoring a configuration closure, we've simplified the setting of the standard Maven coordinates to their bare essence. Both techniques equally shape the output of the JAR file's name and the generated *pom.xml* file contents.

Installing to the Local Maven Repository (Cache)

The Maven plug-in enabled Gradle to not only produce Maven-compatible *pom.xml* and JAR artifacts, but to install those to the local Maven repository. The standard *~/.m2/repository* location is used as the destination, just as it would be from Maven.

Example 4-31. Deploying the Maven-generated artifacts locally

```
$ gradle install

:compileJava
:processResources
:classes
:jar
:install

BUILD SUCCESSFUL
```

This install process, equivalent to `mvn install`, is guaranteed to be compatible with Maven because it actually uses the Maven Ant Tasks (*http://maven.apache.org/ant -tasks/index.html*) produced by the Maven team and hosted at Apache. The *~/.m2/ settings.xml* is consulted, as it would be with Maven, for an alternate location of the default local repository.

Publishing to a Maven Repository

After a successful Gradle build, a binary artifact such as a JAR should be deployed to a binary repository manager such as Artifactory (*http://www.jfrog.com/products.php*) or

Nexus (*http://nexus.sonatype.org/*) for team-wide consumption. Gradle again supports this as simply as its Maven predecessor would with a little configuration of the URL and transport, and then an equivalent to mvn deploy.

As seen in the previous section, the maven plug-in for Gradle offers *pom.xml* and metadata file generation in addition to local installation to the *~/.m2/repository* directory. This plug-in also offers an uploadArchives task that is the equivalent to mvn deploy.

Example 4-32. Gradle build file that permits file:// repository uploads

```
apply plugin: 'java'
apply plugin: 'maven'

group = 'com.gradleware.samples'

uploadArchives {
    repositories.mavenDeployer {
        repository(url: "file:///Users/mccm06/Documents/Temp/Scratch/mytemprepo/")
    }
}
```

Example 4-33. Invoking the artifact upload

```
$ gradle uploadArchives

:clean
:compileJava
:processResources
:classes
:jar
:uploadArchives
Uploading:
 com/gradleware/samples/maven-uploadlocal-unspecified.jar
 to repository remote at
 file:///Users/mccm06/Documents/Temp/Scratch/mytemprepo/
Transferring 1K from remote
Uploaded 1K

BUILD SUCCESSFUL
```

Protocols other than file:// require just slightly more configuration (*http://www.gradle.org/maven_plugin.html*) in that the protocol and wagon JAR that supplies that connectivity must be explicitly called out as shown for webdav in Example 4-34.

Example 4-34. Specifying a webdav protocol for artifact uploads

```
apply plugin: 'java'
apply plugin: 'maven'

group = 'com.gradleware.samples'

configurations {
  deployerJars
}
```

```
repositories {
  mavenCentral()
}

dependencies {
  deployerJars "org.apache.maven.wagon:wagon-webdav-jackrabbit:1.0-beta-7"
}

uploadArchives {
  repositories.mavenDeployer {
    configuration = configurations.deployerJars
    repository(
      url: "http://localhost:8081/nexus/content/repositories/matthew"
    )
  }
}
```

Maven2Gradle Build Script Converter

There is indeed such a tool called maven2gradle (*https://github.com/jbaruch/maven2gra dle*) crafted by Baruch Sadogursky of BMC Software (*http://blog.sadogursky.com/*). It is still under active development on its path to going 1.0, and though young, is useful even in its current form. maven2gradle views the effective-pom flat view of a project's POM as its bridge to export to a Gradle build file. Based on the utility's knowledge of the constrained Maven vocabulary, it converts those instructions to Gradle equivalents.

 The maven2gradle conversion tool is rather sensitive to both the Gradle and Maven tooling versions on the $PATH. Check the project's README for details on tooling version requirements.

The execution of the tool is as simple as cding into a directory containing a standalone or top level multimodule pom.xml file, then executing maven2gradle, as shown in Example 4-35.

Example 4-35. A small Maven POM to be converted to Gradle

```
<!-- The smallest possible Maven POM.xml -->
<project>
  <modelVersion>4.0.0</modelVersion>
  <groupId>com.gradleware.samples</groupId>
  <artifactId>sample01-barestbones</artifactId>
  <version>0.0.1-SNAPSHOT</version>
</project>
```

The tool outputs lightweight progress information as it works through the POM, settings, repositories, dependencies, and WAR natures, as shown in Example 4-36.

Example 4-36. Converting a Maven POM to a Gradle build file

```
$ maven2gradle
Wait, obtaining effective pom... Done.
Wait, obtaining effective settings... Done.
This is single module project.
Configuring Maven repositories... Done.
Configuring Dependencies... Done.
Adding tests packaging...Generating settings.gradle if needed... Done.
Generating main build.gradle... Done.
```

At the conclusion of the tool's execution, a `build.gradle` file and, as needed, a `settings.gradle` file are output to the current working directory. A sample output is shown in Example 4-37.

Example 4-37. The result of the maven2gradle conversion

```
apply plugin: 'java'
apply plugin: 'maven'

  group = 'com.gradleware.samples'
  version = '0.0.1-SNAPSHOT'


description = """"""

sourceCompatibility = 1.5
targetCompatibility = 1.5



repositories {

    mavenRepo urls: ["http://repo1.maven.org/maven2"]
}
```

Taking the file exactly as output by `maven2gradle` would be short of the Gradle build's full potential as it would miss out on some verbosity reductions that Gradle has to offer. The resultant *build.gradle* file will function correctly, but the idea with Gradle is not just to have a functional equivalent in the Groovy language, but a *better* build than what we started with in Maven. The output `build.gradle` can benefit from hand-tuning to leverage more Groovy idioms and Gradle plug-ins. After all, Gradle's aims are to provide you with great possibilities: a more expressive vocabulary and a more concise build file due to the ability to conform to your needs rather than the other way around.

Maven POM Import

A second, and quite different question, is whether Gradle can directly import a Maven POM, capturing the existing behavior and converting it to equivalent Gradle behavior at runtime. The short-term answer is "it's a work in progress" named `Gradle-M2Meta data-Plug-in` (*https://github.com/jbaruch/Gradle-M2Metadata-Plugin*). The limited vocabulary of Maven makes this feasible, but mirroring the idiosyncrasies of Maven's behavior for each combination of tags is a steep challenge. Today, the source compatibility levels, dependencies, coordinates, and packaging can be brought across via a run-time import of a Maven pom.xml file's contents.

To use this plug-in, add an apply and a configuration of the buildScript task that indicates where the plug-in's JAR can be retrieved, as shown in Example 4-38.

Example 4-38. The M2Metadata plug-in's driving build.gradle

```
apply plugin: 'maven-metadata'

//Repo to retrieve the maven-metadata plugin
buildscript {
  repositories {
    mavenRepo urls: ["http://repo.jfrog.org/artifactory/plugins-snapshots"]
  }

  dependencies {
    classpath "org.gradle.plugins:gradle-m2metadata-plugin:1.0-SNAPSHOT"
  }
}
```

On the Maven side, the pom.xml is as traditional as a POM can be. It defines coordinates and two dependencies which are used by the source code. This is shown in Example 4-39.

Example 4-39. The M2Metadata plug-in's consumed pom.xml

```
<!-- The smallest possible Maven POM.xml -->
<project>
  <modelVersion>4.0.0</modelVersion>
  <groupId>com.gradleware.samples</groupId>
  <artifactId>sample01-m2metadata</artifactId>
  <version>0.0.2-SNAPSHOT</version>

  <dependencies>
    <dependency>
        <groupId>log4j</groupId>
        <artifactId>log4j</artifactId>
        <version>1.2.16</version>
    </dependency>
    <dependency>
        <groupId>junit</groupId>
        <artifactId>junit</artifactId>
        <version>4.8.2</version>
        <scope>test</scope>
    </dependency>
  </dependencies>
</project>
```

Conclusion

Gradle, instead of starting anew from the things that we've learned and adopted in the Maven build space, promotes that it is okay to use something that already exists on the way to a better build. Gradle loves scaffolding. Gradle likes convention over configuration. Gradle likes a strong domain model. There's no shame in those similarities to its predecessors. The important twist is that Gradle is willing to be flexible where predecessors would be rigid. This newfound flexibility exists while still facilitating the partial consumption of existing Maven build files for a gradual transition to a full Gradle build. This is certainly the definition of a win-win situation.

CHAPTER 5

Testing with Gradle

The discussion of testing with Gradle takes two primary directions. The first is the simple testing of Java classes with existing test frameworks like JUnit and TestNG. The second is a full automation of the testing pipeline, including separating integration tests from unit test and the leveraging of more advanced testing frameworks like Spock (*http://code.google.com/p/spock/*) and Geb (*http://geb.codehaus.org/latest/index.html*).

JUnit

The simplest JUnit (*http://kentbeck.github.com/junit/*) example is almost entirely supplied by the `java` Gradle plug-in. It adds the `test` task to the build graph and needs only the appropriate JUnit JAR to be added to the classpath to fully activate test execution. This is demonstrated in Example 5-1.

Example 5-1. Testing Java source with JUnit

```
apply plugin: 'java'

repositories {
    mavenCentral()
}

dependencies {
    testCompile 'junit:junit:4.8.2'
}
```

The report from the execution of the JUnit tests is quite handsome compared to its non-Gradle counterparts, as you can see in Figure 5-1. It offers a summary of the tests that were executed, succeeded, and failed.

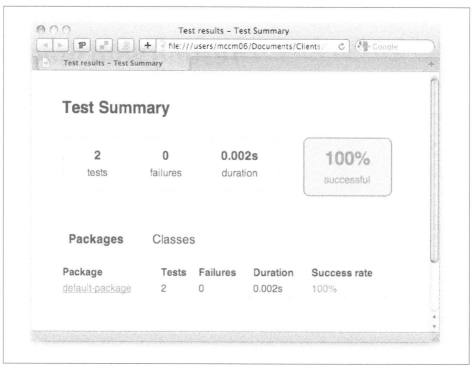

Figure 5-1. JUnit Test Report

When JUnit tests reach a certain level of proliferation within a project, there is a motivation to run them in parallel to get the results faster. However, there would be a great overhead to running *every* unit test in its own JVM. Gradle provides an intelligent compromise in that it offers a `maxParallelForks` that governs the maximum simultaneous JVMs that are spawned.

In the same area of testing, but with a different motivation, is the `forkEvery` setting. Tests, in their quest to touch everything and exercise as much as possible, can cause unnatural pressure on the JVM's memory allocation. In short, it is what Java developers term a "leak". It can merely be the loading of every class causing the problem. This isn't really a leak since the problem stems from the fact that loaded class definitions are not garbage collected but instead are loaded into permgen space. The `forkEvery` setting causes a test-running JVM to close and be replaced by a brand new one after the specified number of tests have run under an instance.

Though these two settings have very different goals, they may often be seen used in combination when a project has a large battery of tests. The use of `forkEvery` and `maxParallelForks` is shown in Example 5-2.

Example 5-2. Testing Java source with multiple JUnit threads

```
apply plugin: 'java'

repositories {
    mavenCentral()
}

dependencies {
    testCompile 'junit:junit:4.8.2'
}

test {
    maxParallelForks = 5
    forkEvery = 50
}
```

In Example 5-2, we leverage the test closure that was provided by the java plug-in as a scoping syntax for assignment of new values to the forkEvery and maxParallelForks variables.

Example 5-3 executes a Gradle build that uses the two governing parallelism settings as set in Example 5-2.

Example 5-3. Displaying the Gradle worker JVMs with the jps utility

```
$ gradle test

:createTests
:compileJava UP-TO-DATE
:processResources UP-TO-DATE
:classes UP-TO-DATE
:compileTestJava
:processTestResources UP-TO-DATE
:testClasses
> Building > :test > 760 tests completed
```

When the Example 5-2 tests should spin up multiple JVMs for unit tests, we can validate this behavior by running the jps command as shown in Example 5-4.

Example 5-4. Displaying the Gradle worker JVMs with the jps utility

```
$ jps

90861 GradleWorkerMain
90862 GradleWorkerMain
90863 GradleWorkerMain
90865 GradleWorkerMain
90864 GradleWorkerMain
90731 GradleMain
```

We can see that five GradleWorkerMain instances are indeed busy, running tests as per our Example 5-2 specifications.

TestNG

A more recent testing framework, TestNG (*http://testng.org/doc/index.html*), has been gaining traction in the Java space as of late. It is also an easy testing framework to use with Gradle. Only the modest addition of the useTestNG() call to the **test** closure is needed in addition to the refactoring of the unit test class.

Example 5-5. A TestNG Unit Test

```
package org.gradle.example.simple;

import org.gradle.example.simple.Person;

import org.testng.annotations.*;
import static org.testng.AssertJUnit.*;

public class TestPerson {
  private Person p = null;

  @BeforeClass
  public void setUp() {
    p = new Person();
        p.setAge(20);
        p.setName("Fird Birfle");
        p.setSalary(195750.22);
  }

  @Test(groups = { "fast" })
  public void testPerson() {
      assertEquals(215325.242, p.calculateBonus(), 0.01);
      assertEquals("The Honorable Fird Birfle", p.becomeJudge());
      assertEquals(30, p.timeWarp());
  }

  @Test(groups = { "slow" })
  public void testPersonAgain() {
        Person p = new Person();
        p.setAge(30);
        p.setName("Bird Firfle");
        p.setSalary(32001.99);

        p.wasteTime();
  }
}
```

Example 5-6. Testing Java source with TestNG

```
apply plugin: 'java'

repositories {
    mavenCentral()
}

test {
```

```
    useTestNG()
}

dependencies {
    testCompile 'org.testng:testng:6.0.1'
}
```

Lastly, when tests start to bifurcate into both unit and integration tests, which among many differentiators, typically means short and long running respectively, a need to also have the tool respect those separations arises. Gradle handles this with aplomb with a simple specification of a pattern of tests to include in each grouping as shown in Example 5-7.

Example 5-7. Separating tests into unit and integration tests

```
apply plugin: 'java'

repositories {
    mavenCentral()
}

dependencies {
    testCompile 'junit:junit:4.8.2'
}

test {
    include '**/Test*.*'
}

task integrationTest(type: Test, dependsOn: "test") << {
    include '**/IntegrationTest*.*'
}
```

This same goal of separating unit and integration tests could also be accomplished with a different technique of separate sourceSet entries. The sourceSet and configuration distinction (one for `unitTest` and one for `integrationTest`) has JAR dependency precision, but also more verbosity. This is similar to the technique employed by the Gradle plug-in in that it has a distinct set of files (*src/main/groovy*) and dependencies (*http://www.gradle.org/groovy_plugin.html*) (like the Groovy core library).

Spock

Spock (*http://code.google.com/p/spock/*), as the homepage states, is a "testing and specification framework for Java and Groovy applications." In a sea of similar tools, it distinguishes itself from the others by a very expressive DSL that reads nearly like natural English writing.

Example 5-8. Spock testing specification

```
class HelloSpock extends spock.lang.Specification {
  def "length of Spock's and his friends' names"() {
```

```
    expect:
    name.size() == length

    where:
    name     | length
    "Spock"  | 5
    "Kirk"   | 4
    "Scotty" | 6
  }
}
```

A Spock specification, since run under the umbrella of JUnit, can be executed by the mere addition of Spock's JAR to Gradle's dependencies.

Example 5-9. Executing Spock test specifications with Gradle

```
apply plugin: "groovy"

repositories {
  mavenCentral()
}

dependencies {
  groovy("org.codehaus.groovy:groovy-all:1.7.5")
  testCompile "org.spockframework:spock-core:0.5-groovy-1.7"

  // dependencies used by examples in this project
  // (not required for using Spock)
  testRuntime "com.h2database:h2:1.2.147"
}
```

The standard results for JUnit executions also apply to Spock, providing a consistent summary of both traditional and specification-style test execution results, as shown in Figure 5-2.

Geb and EasyB

Geb (*http://geb.codehaus.org/latest/index.html*) can be thought of as the furthest reaches of test automation on the JVM with Groovy-based control of web browsers for testing what is primarily thought of as a task for Selenium/WebDriver (*http://code.google.com/p/selenium/wiki/GettingStarted*). There are a growing number of developers writing about (*http://blog.james-carr.org/2011/04/27/using-gebeasyb-with-gradle/*) and demonstrating (*https://github.com/jamescarr/gradle-easyb-geb-example*) this powerful combination of driving a browser from JUnit all the way to specification formats like easyB (*http://www.easyb.org/*).

Gradle can easily drive a Geb and easyB combination with just a few additional dependencies and an Ant task defintion, as shown in Example 5-10.

Default package

all > default-package

31	0	0.317s	100%
tests	failures	duration	successful

Classes

Class	Tests	Failures	Duration	Success rate
DataDriven	4	0	0.003s	100%
DatabaseDriven	1	0	0.070s	100%
DerivedSpec	2	0	0.012s	100%
EmptyStack	4	0	0.040s	100%
HamcrestMatchers	1	0	0.033s	100%
HelloSpock	1	0	0.010s	100%
IncludeExcludeExtension	3	0	0.001s	100%
OrderedInteractions	1	0	0.079s	100%
PublisherSpec	2	0	0.026s	100%
StackWithOneElement	4	0	0.006s	100%
StackWithThreeElements	4	0	0.017s	100%
StepwiseExtension	3	0	0s	100%
UsingJUnitRules	1	0	0.020s	100%

Generated by Gradle 1.0-milestone-3 at May 25, 2011 5:06:36 PM

Figure 5-2. JUnit test report for Spock tests

Example 5-10. Geb Gradle build file

```
apply plugin: 'groovy'

repositories {
    mavenCentral()
}

dependencies {
//    groovy 'org.codehaus.groovy:groovy:1.7.10'
    testCompile ('org.easyb:easyb:0.9.8')
        testCompile 'org.codehaus.geb:geb-core:0.5.1'
        testCompile 'org.codehaus.geb:geb-easyb:0.5.1'
        testCompile 'org.seleniumhq.selenium:selenium-htmlunit-driver:2.0a7'
}

test.doLast {
    ant.taskdef(name: "easyb", classname:"org.easyb.ant.BehaviorRunnerTask", classpath:
        sourceSets.test.runtimeClasspath.asPath)

    ant.easyb( classpath: sourceSets.test.runtimeClasspath.asPath,
        failureProperty:'easyb_failed' ) {
        report( location:"${project.testResultsDir}/story.html", format:"html" )
        behaviors( dir: "src/test/stories" ) {
            include( name:"**/*.story" )
        }
    }

    ant.fail( if:'easyb_failed', message: 'Failures in easyb stories')
}
```

The easyB specification file reads like plain English in its execution of web browser driving events and querying of the page responses.

Example 5-11. Geb easyB specification

```
using "geb"

scenario "scripting style", {

    when "we go to google", {
        go "http://google.com"
    }

    then "we are at google", {
        page.title.shouldBe "Google"
    }

    when "we search for chuck", {
        $("input", name: "q").value("chuck norris")
        $("input", value: "Google Search").click()
    }

    then "we are now at the results page", {
        page.title.shouldEndWith "Google Search"
```

```
    }
    and "we get straight up norris", {
        $("li.g", 0).find("a.l").text().shouldStartWith "Chuck Norris"
    }
}
```

And, at the end of the Geb via easyB execution, a very pleasant results page (Figure 5-3) describes the stories that were run, like a richer version of the JUnit test report.

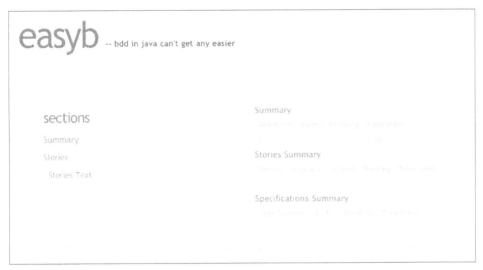

Figure 5-3. easyB test report for Geb tests

Gradle's Testing Focus

The review and examples of testing with Gradle shows that the traditional JUnit testing approach is slightly less ceremonious than with other build tools. However, Gradle truly shines in that the more advanced forms of separating integration tests, running Spock specifications, or driving the browser via Geb are handled with absolutely simplicity. As more complex software, larger code bases, and increased automation drive developers toward these more advanced testing tools, Gradle is poised to offer the most convenient use. This will continue to drive Gradle's adoption as a software craftsperson's build and automation tool.

CHAPTER 6

Multiproject Builds

Large projects are typically broken up into separate modules with independent build lifecycles. Each subproject has some kind of life of its own, perhaps with a development team assigned to it alone, and certainly with a test suite of its own which is worthwhile to run apart from the project as a whole. However, any large system that is broken into pieces must also be reintegrated together, implying the need for a master build that combines all subprojects into a single integration test suite and set of release artifacts or processes. A next-generation build system will be equipped to provide a flexible framework for dealing with real-world project differentiation and integration.

Multiproject Build Structure

A multiproject is generally hierarchical in nature: it typically has a master project with one or more subprojects. In some cases, subprojects may be nested. The master project goes in a top-level directory, with subprojects arranged in subdirectories underneath. The master project may add code, resources, tests, and build conventions of its own, or it may simply be build glue that holds the project tree together.

In the most intuitive case, Gradle allows you to define a build file for the top-level project and one for each subproject. In a more interesting and potentially more useful case, it also lets you define the entire build from the top-level build file. Alternatively, if neither a scattered set of individual build files nor a single, integrated build file suits you, you can also put some build configuration in the top-level build file and put project-specific details in the project-specific build files in their respective subdirectories. As usual, Gradle wants to you give you the ability to define your own build conventions, rather than impose its opinions on you.

To tell Gradle which subdirectories of the root project actually contain projects (and not merely sources or build outputs), you must provide the `settings.gradle` file. This is a build configuration file which is independent of `build.gradle`. In the simplest case, `settings.gradle` simply lists the names of the subdirectories which contain subprojects, and nothing more.

When Gradle runs the Initialization lifecycle phase, it first looks for `settings.gradle`, and from it finds the list of subdirectories which contain subprojects. If those subdirectories contain `build.gradle` files of their own, they are processed next and incorporated into the directed acyclic graph (DAG) that describes the build. The fact that Gradle is building an internal project DAG reveals a compelling option: given the right Gradle syntax, we can actually do all of the multiproject build configuration from a single build.gradle file at the root level. We can also distribute all of the configuration to the individual build files, or use a hybrid approach in which common configuration settings are in the master file, and project-specific settings reside in the individual build files.

Project-Specific Build Files

Having a single, project-specific build file per subproject is easiest to digest for most new users. There is a `settings.gradle` file at the project root, and a `build.gradle` file at the root and in each subproject directory. Each subproject manages its own build affairs, and the top-level project combines the subproject build outputs into the integrated build outcome which is the ultimate goal of the build.

In our example, the root project is a command-line application that takes the name of a poet as a command line argument, then emits a few lines of that poet's poetry to the console in an encoded form. One of its dependencies is a project containing a simple API for generating the poems, including a Java interface, a factory class, and several implementations containing different poem fragments. The other dependency is an API that encodes arbitrary strings first with the Metaphone algorithm, then the Base64 format. The top-level application has the responsibility of calling both APIs to emit encoded poetry to the console. This example illustrates two dependent subprojects, one of which is a completely standalone API, and one of has external JAR dependencies which must be fetched from an online repository and made available to the root-level project.

The `settings.gradle` file looks as shown in Example 6-1.

Example 6-1. The settings.gradle file for a simple multiproject build.

```
include 'codec', 'content'
```

This is the most basic use of `settings.gradle` possible. It simply names the subprojects by directory name, relative to the directory of the top-level project. The `settings.gradle` file is interpreted during the Initialization lifecycle phase, when the skeleton of the build graph is being constructed. Consequently, a richer API than the include method is available. In general, any part of the Gradle API that affects the structure of the build graph can be called in this file. We haven't looked in detail at what these API calls are yet, but later on in this chapter, we'll look at some of them when we extract parts of the subproject build files into the top-level build file.

The top-level build file looks as shown in Example 6-2.

Example 6-2. The root project build file, when subprojects have individual build files

```
evaluationDependsOn(':codec')

apply plugin: 'java'

dependencies {
  compile project(':codec')
  compile project(':content')
}

[ 'shakespeare', 'williams', 'shelley', 'chesterton' ].each { poet -> ❶
  task "${poet}"(type: JavaExec) { ❷
    group = 'Encoded Poetry'
    args = [ poet ] ❸
    main = 'org.gradle.example.codedpoet.CommandLine'
    classpath sourceSets.main.runtimeClasspath,
              project(':codec').sourceSets.main.runtimeClasspath
  }
}
```

❶ This Groovy code declares a list of four strings (each of which is the name of a poet), then iterates over that list.

❷ This line creates a dynamic task in the top-level project named after each poet.

❸ The `args` parameter expects a `List`, so we use Groovy list literal syntax to wrap the `poet` variable.

There are a few things in this build file that we haven't seen yet. First of all, note that the dependencies aren't vectors describing a JAR file in a repository, but they are projects. The `project()` method queries the Gradle DAG and returns the project object belonging to a subproject. The colon at the beginning of the project name indicates the root of the project tree, in a similar way that a forward slash indicates the root directory in a Unix filesystem, or a backslash indicates the root directory on Windows. The project name following the colon is the project name as given in `settings.gradle`. This top-level project's dependencies block indicates that it depends on the `codec` and `content` subprojects.

This build file also uses dynamic task creation. The dynamic tasks created in this build file are `JavaExec` tasks, each of which runs the `org.gradle.example.codedpoet.Command Line` class, passing in the name of the poet as a command-line argument. Most importantly, each task's classpath property is given two arguments: the `runtimeClasspath` of the top-level project, and the `runtimeClasspath` of the `:codec` project.

The codec project's classpath must be added to the `JavaExec` task explicitly because the codec introduces a dependency of its own: namely, the Apache commons-codec library. It is very typical for subprojects to have their own dependencies, either stored locally in the project or retrieved from a Maven- or Ivy-style repository, so including them in the top-level project's build is commonplace.

Finally, the first line of `build.gradle` introduces a method call we have not seen before. The `evaluationDependsOn()` method, which takes a subproject name as its argument, indicates that the evaluation of the current project (the top-level or root project) depends on the named project. This method call is necessary to enable the dependencies of the codec project to be available in the top-level project. Calling this method will always force the named project to be evaluated first, so its contributions to the project graph will exist before the current project is evaluated.

The build file of the content project is trivial (Example 6-3).

Example 6-3. The build file of the content subproject.

```
apply plugin: 'java'
```

It is a pure Java project with no external dependencies, following all of the conventions of the Java plug-in. The code itself is only slightly more complex, having an interface, a factory class, and several concrete implementations of the interface. These are all compiled and bundled into a JAR to be used by the top-level project.

The build file of the codec project contains only slightly more configuration (Example 6-4).

Example 6-4. The build file of the codec subproject.

```
apply plugin: 'java'

repositories {
  mavenCentral()
}

dependencies {
  compile 'commons-codec:commons-codec:1.5'
}
```

In addition to applying the Java plug-in, it also names Maven Central as a repository, and declares the Apache commons-codec library version 1.5 as a dependency. The code itself declares a single class called `Encoder`, which exposes a method that calls both the Metaphone and Base64 codecs on a string argument.

Splitting a multiproject build into a parent project and multiple subprojects, and giving each subproject its own build file, is an easy-to-understand structure with much to recommend it as a standard approach to complex, composite Gradle projects. However, the fact that Gradle converts the build files internally into a unified project DAG exposes a couple of other options for us when deciding how to organize multiproject builds. Let's look at how we might refactor this build to put all of the build configuration into one file.

One Master Build File

The previous multiproject build can be expressed in a single build file in the root project. The `settings.gradle` remains the same, naming the subprojects by their directories (Example 6-5).

Example 6-5. The settings.gradle for the unified multiproject build case.

```
include 'codec', 'content'
```

However, the `build.gradle` files in the `codec` and `content` subproject directories go away entirely. They are replaced with configuration in the master build file (Example 6-6).

Example 6-6. A unified build file for a mutli-project build

```
evaluationDependsOn(':codec')  ❶

allprojects {  ❷
  apply plugin: 'java'
}

project(':codec') {  ❸
  repositories {
    mavenCentral()
  }

  dependencies {
    compile 'commons-codec:commons-codec:1.5'
  }
}

dependencies {
  compile project(':codec')
  compile project(':content')
}

[ 'shakespeare', 'williams', 'shelley', 'chesterton' ].each { poet ->
  task "${poet}"(type: JavaExec) {
    group = 'Encoded Poetry'
    args = [ poet ]
    main = 'org.gradle.example.codedpoet.CommandLine'
    classpath sourceSets.main.runtimeClasspath,
              project(':codec').sourceSets.main.runtimeClasspath
  }
}
```

❶ The call to `evaluationDependsOn()` tells Gradle to evaluate the `:codec` build file before the root project's build file. This ensure that `codec` build objects will exist in the graph before the rest of this build file is evaluated.

❷ The `allprojects` method passes all of its configuration to all projects in the build, including the root and all subprojects.

❸ The project() method gives us direct access to the configuration of the codec sub-project. Using this syntax, we can configure any project in the graph.

In the unified build, all three projects need the Java plug-in, so we apply that plug-in inside the allprojects closure. If we had configuration to apply only to subprojects, we could use the subprojects method instead.

The codec project has some individual configuration needs that don't apply to the other two projects in the build, and we can apply this configuration by using the project() method. Note that the parameter passed to project() is :codec. Using this syntax, we can access the project graph of any configured subproject. The power and flexibility of this syntax is difficult to overstate. The object returned by project() is a Project object, which is implicitly the object being operated on by all of the methods normally called in a Gradle build file. Just as repositories and dependencies are configured in this block, tasks could be created or modified, new Java SourceSets defined, plug-ins applied, or any other Gradle configuration operation performed. The ability to access the Project object from the top-level build file gives us complete control over the structure of the entire build. This feature is much more consequential than its ordinary-seeming syntax would suggest.

The rest of the build file is the same as what we saw in the individual build file example: the root project is made to depend on the two subprojects, and a set of tasks is dynamically created to call the CommandLine class with an appropriate argument. This gives us the same functionality as the individual build file example.

A Hybrid Multiproject Build

So far, we've seen two ways of expressing a multiproject build: splitting the build up into several project-specific build files, and combining all build configuration into one master build file. As an alternative to these, you may find that the most expressive way to describe your build is to choose a hybrid approach in which some configuration is placed in the root build file and some is included in project-specific build files. Let's rework the build files from the previous two examples to reflect such a hybrid config-uration.

The new root-level build file still contains an allprojects configuration, applying the Java plug-in to all projects. Otherwise, it looks just like the root project build file from the individual build file example. The resulting file is shown in Example 6-7.

Example 6-7. The build file of the root-level project in the hybrid multiproject build case.

```
allprojects {
  apply plugin: 'java'
}

evaluationDependsOn(':codec')

dependencies {
```

```
  compile project(':codec')
  compile project(':content')
}

[ 'shakespeare', 'williams', 'shelley', 'chesterton' ].each { poet ->
  task "${poet}"(type: JavaExec) {
    group = 'Encoded Poetry'
    args = [ poet ]
    main = 'org.gradle.example.codedpoet.CommandLine'
    classpath sourceSets.main.runtimeClasspath,
    project(':codec').sourceSets.main.runtimeClasspath
  }
}
```

Since the dependency and repository configuration of the codec project were specific to that project, we push that configuration back down into its build file as shown in Example 6-8:

Example 6-8. The build file for the codec subproject.

```
repositories {
  mavenCentral()
}

dependencies {
  compile 'commons-codec:commons-codec:1.5'
}
```

Note that we do not apply the Java plug-in in the code project's build file, since the Java plug-in is a common configuration step that is done in the root-level build.gra dle file. Because of this, there is no need to provide a build file for the content subproject, since that very simple build relies entirely on the defaults provided by the Java plug-in, which is applied by the root project.

Individual, Unified, or Hybrid?

The three approaches we've explored here each have unique advantages. Creating a single build file for each subproject project provides for a very clear separation of concerns, and is a very easy-to-understand approach for new users of Gradle. Putting all configuration into a single build file puts the entire description of the build in one easy-to-examine file. A hybrid approach lets us put common configuration in one place, then to factor project-specific configuration into build files associated with their individual projects. Each one of these approaches has something to recommend it.

Each is desirable for a reason of its own, but Gradle imposes no opinion on which approach is correct. As a user of Gradle, you are free to structure your multiproject builds in whatever way best fits your circumstances and build sensibilities.

Multiproject Task Structure

Gradle considers a multi-project build as a single graph of projects, tasks, and other configuration data structures. As a result, running the build from inside the root project or any subproject gives you access to the entire graph of tasks. If you're in the directory of a subproject, you don't have to change directories into another subproject to get access to that project's tasks.

The task addressing scheme is similar to directory paths in the file system, except it uses colons instead of slashes as delimiters. A colon at the beginning of a fully qualified task name indicates the root project. If the colon is followed by the name of the task in the root project, then that fully qualified task name refers to that task in the root project —whether Gradle is being executed from within the root directory or from within a subproject directory. If the text after the colon is a subproject name, then it should be followed by another colon and the name of a task within that subproject. Again, this task can be invoked no matter what project directory in the tree you're in when you run Gradle.

If you want to run the whole project build while in the directory of a subproject, you might use the command line shown in Example 6-9.

Example 6-9. Running a task in the root project from within a subproject directory

```
[~/mutiproject] $ cd codec
[~/mutiproject/codec] $ gradle :build
:codec:compileJava
:codec:processResources
:codec:classes
:codec:jar
:content:compileJava
:content:processResources
:content:classes
:content:jar
:compileJava
:processResources
:classes
:jar
:assemble
:compileTestJava
:processTestResources
:testClasses
:test
:check
:build

BUILD SUCCESSFUL

Total time: 12.333 secs
```

If you want to build another subproject while in one subproject's directory, you'd use the longer task syntax (Example 6-10).

Example 6-10. Running one subproject's tasks while in a second subproject

```
[~/mutiproject] $ cd content
[~/mutiproject/content] $ gradle :codec:compileJava
:codec:compileJava

BUILD SUCCESSFUL

Total time: 1.274 secs
```

This same syntax applies when you're in the root project and want to run a subproject task directly, except that you may optionally omit the colon, since you're already at the root level (Example 6-11).

Example 6-11. Running a subproject task from the root project

```
[~/mutiproject] $ gradle codec:jar
:codec:compileJava
:codec:processResources
:codec:classes
:codec:jar

BUILD SUCCESSFUL

Total time: 0.996 secs
```

Multiple Projects Your Way

Gradle's internal architecture lends itself to a very fluid way of dealing with multiproject builds. It is a central fact of Gradle's architecture that it converts all build.gradle files into a unified DAG that describes the dependencies and associated actions of a build. The existence of this DAG gives you tremendous flexibility in how you want to represent the configuration of your multiproject build in your actual project files. The individual, unified, and hybrid approaches—all of which are automatically integrated by the time the build executes—offer options that should appeal to all build developers regardless of project structure and developer preferences. As usual, Gradle wants to provide you with the tools to create your own standards, rather than impose its standards on you.

About the Authors

Tim is a full-stack generalist and passionate teacher who loves coding, presenting, and working with people. He is founder and principal software developer at the August Technology Group, a technology consulting firm focused on the JVM. He is a speaker internationally and on the No Fluff Just Stuff tour in the United States, copresenter of the best-selling O'Reilly Git Master Class, and is copresident of the Denver Open Source User Group. He has recently been exploring build automation, nonrelational data stores, and abstract ideas like how to make software architecture look more like an ant colony. He lives in Littleton, CO, with the wife of his youth and their three children.

Matthew is an energetic fifteen-year veteran of enterprise software development, world-traveling open source educator, and co-founder of Ambient Ideas, LLC, a U.S. consultancy. Matthew currently is a trainer for Gradleware, educator for GitHub.com, author of the Git Master Class series for O'Reilly, speaker on the No Fluff Just Stuff tour, author of three of the top ten DZone RefCards (including the Git RefCard), and President of the Denver Open Source Users Group. His current topics of research center around project automation, including: build tools (Gradle, Leiningen, Maven, Ant), distributed version control (Git, Mercurial), testing frameworks (Geb, Spock, JUnit, TestNG, Mockito), continuous integration (Jenkins, Hudson, Bamboo) and code quality metrics (Sonar, CodeNarc, PMD).

Colophon

The animal on the cover of *Building and Testing with Gradle*, first edition, is a bush wren.

The cover image is from *Cassell's Natural History*. The cover font is Adobe ITC Garamond. The text font is Linotype Birka; the heading font is Adobe Myriad Condensed; and the code font is LucasFont's TheSansMonoCondensed.

Get even more for your money.

Join the O'Reilly Community, and register the O'Reilly books you own. It's free, and you'll get:

- $4.99 ebook upgrade offer
- 40% upgrade offer on O'Reilly print books
- Membership discounts on books and events
- Free lifetime updates to ebooks and videos
- Multiple ebook formats, DRM FREE
- Participation in the O'Reilly community
- Newsletters
- Account management
- 100% Satisfaction Guarantee

Signing up is easy:

1. **Go to: oreilly.com/go/register**
2. **Create an O'Reilly login.**
3. **Provide your address.**
4. **Register your books.**

Note: English-language books only

To order books online:
oreilly.com/store

For questions about products or an order:
orders@oreilly.com

To sign up to get topic-specific email announcements and/or news about upcoming books, conferences, special offers, and new technologies:
elists@oreilly.com

For technical questions about book content:
booktech@oreilly.com

To submit new book proposals to our editors:
proposals@oreilly.com

O'Reilly books are available in multiple DRM-free ebook formats. For more information:
oreilly.com/ebooks

Spreading the knowledge of innovators   oreilly.com

The information you need, when and where you need it.

With Safari Books Online, you can:

Access the contents of thousands of technology and business books

- Quickly search over 7000 books and certification guides
- Download whole books or chapters in PDF format, at no extra cost, to print or read on the go
- Copy and paste code
- Save up to 35% on O'Reilly print books
- **New!** Access mobile-friendly books directly from cell phones and mobile devices

Stay up-to-date on emerging topics before the books are published

- Get on-demand access to evolving manuscripts.
- Interact directly with authors of upcoming books

Explore thousands of hours of video on technology and design topics

- Learn from expert video tutorials
- Watch and replay recorded conference sessions

9 781449 304638